Genée, Richard; Riegen, J.; Czibulka, Alfons

Whitsuntide in Florence

Inktank publishing

Genée, Richard; Riegen, J.; Czibulka, Alfons

Whitsuntide in Florence

Inktank publishing, 2018

www.inktank-publishing.com

ISBN/EAN: 9783747772836

Richard Genée and J. Riegen.

MUSIC BY

ALFONS CZIBULKA

Vocal Score 1.00	Potpourri *Blake* .75	Galop *Thorne* .35
Piano Score .50	Angelo Waltzes *Czibulka* .75	March ... *Himelman* .35
Mandolina . *Serenade Vocal* .50	Gems .25	Mandolina. *Serenade for Pianoforte* .35

WHITE, SMITH & CO.
BOSTON *Copyright, 1886, by White, Smith & Co.* CHICAGO

PRELUDE.

Allegro brillante. 𝅗𝅥= 132.

CZIBULKA.

pp m. g.
tr
8
ff
p
m. g.
pp
Cadenza.
Andante. ♩=72.
p
mf
dim.
rit.
cresc.
espress.
trem.
3
pp

No 1. INTRODUCTION.
Vivace.
ANGELO.
CHOR
SOPRAN.
TENOR.
BASS.
Vivace. ♩=126.
PIANO.
TEN.
Yes to-day the mar-ket's ris-ing, And some
Fried-lich lacht der Markt noch heu-te; ob's auch
BASS.
Yes to-day the mar-ket's ris-ing, And some
Fried-lich lacht der Markt noch heu-te; ob's auch
mon-ey can be made, Still the fact there's no dis-guis-ing,
mor-gen so wird sein? Un-ter ste-tem Kampf und Strei-te,
mon-ey can be made, Still the fact there's no dis-guis-ing,
mor-gen so wird sein? Un-ter ste-tem Kampf und Strei-te,

6
All these rows are bad for trade, Con-stant rows are bad for
kann der Han-del nicht ge-deih'n kann der Han-del nicht ge-
All these rows are bad for trade, Con-stant rows are bad for
kann der Han-del nicht ge-deih'n kann der Han-del nicht ge-
L'istesso Tempo.
SOP. I.
trade. FRAUEN. Whitsuntide is nigh, So bid all care good-bye, No
deih'n! Pfingsten ist schon nah, das schö-ne Fest ist da, und
SOP. II.
trade Whit-sun-tide is nigh, So bid all care good-bye, No
deih'n! Pfingsten ist schon nah, das schö-ne Fest ist da, und
L'istesso Tempo.
feast is half so gay, For win-ter's fled a-way. And in joyous Spring Each
wie sichs da-bei schickt, prangt Al-les grün geschmückt Bald die Lust be-ginnt, drum
feast is half so gay, For win-ter's fled a-way, And in joyous Spring
wie sichs da-bei schickt, prangt Al-les grün geschmückt Bald die Lust beginnt.
heart must laugh and sing, Ev-e-ry care will from us glide, At Whitsuntide.
eilt, die Zeit verrinnt? Mor-gen soll man Al-les schön im Glanze seh'n!
Each heart must laugh and sing, Ev-e-ry care will from us glide, At Whitsuntide.
drum eilt, die Zeit ver-rinnt? Mor-gen soll man Al-les schön im Glanze seh'n!

L'istesso Tempo.
FRAUEN.
SOP. I. II.
Yes, to - day the Mar - ket's ri - sing, And some mon - ey can be
Friedlich lacht der Markt noch heu - te, und so soll es mor - gen
MÄNNER.
TENOR.
Yes, to - day the Mar - ket's ri - sing, And some mon - ey can be
Fried und Freu - de la - chen heu - te, ob's auch mor - gen so wird
BASS.
L'istesso Tempo.
made; Still the fact there's no dis - guis - ing: End - less rows are
sein? Lasst die Po - li - tik bei Sei - te, heit're Lust nur
made; Still the fact there's no dis - guis - ing: End - less rows are
sein? Un - ter ste - tem Kampf und Strei - te, kann der Han - del
bad for trade, End - less rows are bad for trade.
herrsch' al - lein, heit're Lust nur herrsch' al - lein!
bad for trade, End - less rows are bad for trade.
nicht ge - deih'n, kann der Han - del nicht ge - deih'n!

cres. poco a poco
Buy then, buy then, Our wares try then, For to - mor - row's ho - li -
Kau - fet, kau - fet, ei - let, kau - fet, mor - gen winkt ein Fei - er -
Buy then, buy then, Our wares try then, For to - mor - row's ho - li -
Kau - fet, kau - fet, ei - let, kau - fet, mor - gen winkt ein Fei - er -
cres. po - co a po - co
- day. Fling all sor - row off to - mor - row, Let your hearts be
- tag! Heut' in Sor - gen, treibt es mor - gen Je - der fröh - lich
- day. Fling all sor - row off to - mor - row, Let your hearts be
- tag! Heut' in Sor - gen, treibt es mor - gen Je - der fröh - lich
light and gay.
wie er mag.
light and gay. Let your po - li - tics be end - ed, For they
wie er mag. Un - ter ste - tem Kampf und Strei - te kann der

Let your pol-i-tics be end-ed, Let your pol-i-ties be ended,
Lasst die Po-li-tik bei Sei-te, lass die Po-li-tik bei Sei-te,
drive all trade a-way, Let your pol-i-ties be end-ed,
Han-del nicht ge-deih'n! Un-ter ste-tem Kampf und Strei-te
Mirth a-lone shall rule to-day, Mirth a-lone shall rule to-day. Mirth a-
heit're Lust nur herrsch' al-lein, heit're Lust nur herrsch' al-lein, heit're
for they drive all trade a-way, For they drive all trade a-way, For they
kann der Han-del nicht ge-deih'n, kann der Han-del nicht ge-deih'n, kann der
-lone shall rule to-day.
Lust nur herrsch' al-lein!
drive all trade a-way.
Han-del nicht ge-deih'n!
ANGELO (enters.)
(Fanfare be-hind the scenes.)
morendo.

Melodram.
(Fanfare on the stage.)
Allegretto moderato.
pp
L'istesso Tempo.
ANGELO (aside.)
Though banished from the State, Yet I have dared here to show me, Here for Ri - ta I'll
Oh aus der Stadt ver - bannt, wagt ich mich doch ein - zu - schleichen hier im frem - dem Ge -
(Fanfare behind the scenes.)
p
L'istesso Tempo.
p
pp stacc.

A
wait! In this garb I'm sure none will know me,
wand Möch - te Ri - ta ge - ben ein Zei - chen
Though still the dan-ger is great, I hope to pass quite safe in the crowd,
noch hat mich Niemand er - kannt. Dass die Verklei - dung man nicht durchschaut,
md.
pp
tr
fz
If I but cry my wares a - loud; This low dis-guise will
preis' ich jetzt mei - ne Waa - re laut; dass die Ver - klei - dung
do ve-ry well, But I my waves must loud - ly yell, Come buy here! Come
man nicht durchschaut, preis' ich jetzt mei - ne Waa - re laut; Com-pra - te! Com -
ff (screaming.)
tr
fz
buy here! Come buy now! Come buy now!
pra te! Com-pra - te! Com-pra - te!
ff
Some Women. f
What would you here?
Was will er hier?
Some Men. Here stop your noise.
Was schreit der Bursch?
f
f

12
A
Come buy my figures they're not dear! I'll sell you here a love-ly
Kauft die Fi-guren doch von mir! Ein hoch berühmt es Lie-bes-
pair, 'Tis Petrarch and his own Lau-ra fair. Come
paar! Pe-trar-ca mit Lau-ra biet' ich dar! Com-
buy now! Come buy now! (aside.) If she'd on-ly once come
pra-te! Com-pra-te! Wenn sie in der Näh' doch
near, Come buy now! Come buy now!
wär'! Com-pra-te! Com-pra-te!
WHOLE CHORUS.
Hush! and say what would you here?
Schweig'! Und sag' wo kommst du her?
Hush! and say what would you here?
Schweig'! Und sag' wo kommst du her?

Moderato. 𝅗𝅥=76.
1. Came from the Pon-te del-le Gra-zie, Where not a bit of luck I had, Then to the Pla-za Lig-nori-a, There 'twas the same, Bus'-ness is bad.
2. Then I went on the Lungar-no, Saw lots of peo-ple rich-ly clad, But not a soul would spend a copper, It's just my luck, Bus'-ness is bad.
1. Kom-me von pon te-del-le gra-zie, wo mei-ne Waar' ich aus-ge-stellt, war auch am Platz der Lig-no-ri-a, nir-gend Geschäft! nir-gend ist Geld!
2. Ging dann ent-lang dem Lun-gar-no, wo ihr die reich-sten Leu-te trefft, doch für die Kunst will Niemand zahlen; nir-gend Geschäft! nir-gend ist Geld!
TENOR.
Yes it is sad, Bus'-ness is bad, Bus'-ness is bad.
Nir-gend Geschäft! Nir-gend ist Geld! Nir-gend ist Geld!
BASS.
(among themselves.)
Ah! too well we know, Just why it is so,
Wir wis-sen's wa-rum! Und dul-den es stumm!

Vivace.
Fra Bombarda's ir - on sway. Soon I think will pass a - way.
Fra Bombarda's Re - gi - ment, geht, so scheint mir, bald zu End!
Vivace. ♩=126.
p colla parte.
ff
Come
Con -
WOMEN.
Let your pol - i - ties be end - ed, Mirth a - lone shall rule to -
Lasst die Po - li - tik bei Sei - te, heu - te herr - sche Lust al -
TENOR.
MEN.
Let your pol - i - ties be end - ed, Mirth a - lone shall rule to -
Bei dem ite - ten Kampf und Strei - te, kann der Han - del nicht ge -
BASS.
L'isstesso Tempo.
buy now, Come buy now! Come buy my figures of
pa - te! Com - pa - te! Kauft die Fi - gu - ren von
day. Hush! No more would we hear, No more would we hear!
Schweig! Wir ha - ben's ge - hört, wir ha - bens ge - hört!
day. Hush! No more would we hear, No more would we hear!
deihn! Schweig! Wir ha - ben's ge - hört, wir ha - bens ge - hört!
L'isstesso Tempo.
ff
p colla

A
match-less worth Pe - trarch and Lau - ra, And if you wish ___ to
ho - hem Werth! Lau - ra Pe - trar - ca! Wenn ihr's be - gehrt, ___ wohl -
f
p
pp
A
listen. to their sto - ry, I'll tell you of their glo - ry,
an denn, so be - rich - te ich da - zu die Ge - schich - te!
Yes, yes, tell the
Ja, ja, die Ge -
Yes, yes, tell the
Ja, ja, die Ge -
sto - ry, Yes tell us the sto - ry, Come and hear, let all give ear.
schich - te! Be - rich - te; be - rich - te! Schweigt und hört ja, schweigt und hört!
sto - ry, Yes tell us the sto - ry, Come and hear, let all give ear.
schich - te! Be - rich - te, be - rich - te! Schweigt und hört ja, schweigt und hört!
6173 + 101

16 Couplet.
Moderato.
1. Once Petrarch loved his pret-ty
works were eve-ry where much
1. Pe-trar-ca lieb-te sei-ne
fei-ert war durch ganz I-
Moderato. ♩= 72.
Lau-ra, His heart he gave un-to her care; So much this lov-er did a-
lauded, All oth-er son-nets seem but faint, His love was ver-y much ap-
Lau-ra, sie nahm das gan-ze Herz ihm ein; er dich-te-te im sie So-
ta-lien Pe-trar-ca's Dich-ter ge-ni-us; man weih-te ihm die Lor-beer-
dore her, He wrote her ten-der ver-ses rare. For her a-lone his pen was
plauded, They ev-en made of him a saint; He prais'd his Lau-ra's wit and
net-te, die heut' noch al-le Welt er-freu'n. Für sie nur schrieb er sei-ne
kro-ne, auch wur-de er Ka-no-ni-kus! Und da-bei pries er Lau-ra's
writing, He sent her poems from near and far, Which eve-ry heart are still de-
beauty, And eve-ry day he new be-gan, But af-ter he had done this
Lieder, für sie nur schwärmte er von fern, sie strahlt bei Ta-ge ihm als
Rei-ze, in tau-send Rei-men min-nig-lich, al-lein die Da-me war sehr
ritard.
Mosso. ♩= 132.
lighting, All this he did for his bright star! Yet e'en 'mid his ten-der-est prais-
du-ty, She wedded with some oth-er man. Twelve children the fair Lau-ra nurs-
Son-ne, und funkel-te ihm Nachts als Stern! Doch nie war's dem Dichter be-schie-
praktisch, nahm lieber ei-nen Gat-ten sich! Der E-he war Se-gen be-schie-
Copyright, 1885, by White, Smith & Co.

ing, His star from a distance he'd see; Not even a kiss he was
es, She'd infants a dozen you see; Yet he did not load her with
den, zu nah'n seinem Sterne so licht; ihm blühte kein Küsschen hie-
den: Zwölf Kinder, so sagt der Bericht; der Dichter, der gab sich zu-
ritard.
Allegretto.
raising, And he was content with mere gazing. We would not be!
curses, Oh no! but he wrote her more verses So would not we!
nieden, er war mit dem Anschaun zufrieden, wir wären's nicht!
frieden, fuhr fort, ihr Sonette zu schmieden, wir thuen's nicht!
ritard.
Allegretto. ♩ = 112.
mf
fz
A
We would not be!
So would not we!
Wir wären's nicht!
Wir thuen's nicht!
ff
We would not be, We would not be!
So would not we, So would not we!
Wir wären's nicht wir wären's nicht!
Wir thäten's nicht wir thäten's nicht!
Gelächter.
ff
We would not be, We would not be!
So would not we, So would not we!
Wir wären's nicht wir wären's nicht!
Wir thäten's nicht wir thäten's nicht!
fz
f
ff
A
1.
2.
2. His
2. Ge.
fz
ffz

№ 2. Chorus of Guardsmen.

6173-191

cresc. al f

F

Ev'-ry burgher rul-ing, We from them permit no fool-ing, 'Tis their humble-
Strei-fel durch die Gas-sen, las-set nimmer mit Euch spas-sen, denn der Bür-ger

Ev'-ry burgher rul-ing, We from them permit no fool-ing, 'Tis their humble
Strei-fel durch die Gas-sen, las-set nimmer mit Euch spas-sen, denn der Bür-ger

p

cresc. al f

F

ff

task to give us, whatso-e'er we ask, We rule with ease these stu-pid
giebt, was an-zu-nehmen uns be-liebt! Wir wis-sen uns Re-spekt zu

ff

task to give us, whatso-e'er we ask, We rule with ease these stu-pid
giebt, was an-zu-nehmen uns be-liebt! Wir wis-sen uns Re-spekt zu

ff

f

ff

F

cat-tle, We know it well, ——— None dare re-bel, If they pro-
schaf-fen, man wagt kein Wort, ——— gehorcht so fort. Im star-ker

cat-tle, We know it well, ——— None dare re-bel, If they pro-
schaf-fen, man wagt kein Wort, ——— gehorcht so fort. Im star-ker

F
-test, our swords we rat - tle, And then at once they're dumb beneath our
Hand führ'n wir die Waf - fen. Ein Blick von uns ge - nügt, dass man sich
-test, our swords we rat - tle, And then at once they're dumb beneath our
Hand - führ'n wir die Waf - fen, Ein Blick von uns ge - nügt, dass man sich
fz
3
F
thumb, Yes, then at once they're dumb beneath our thumb!
fügt, ein Blick von uns ge - nügt, dass man sich fügt!
thumb, Yes, then at once they're dumb beneath our thumb!
fügt, ein Blick von uns ge - nügt, dass man sich fügt!
fz
fz
F
fz
fz
If in du - ty they are fail - ing, Let your swords ap -
Wenn sie mur - ren, wenn sie grol - len, lo - ckert nur das
p
fz
fz
F
f
fz
p
fz
- pear, Let your swords ap - pear. Ah! it has
Schwert, lo - ckert nur das Schwert. Und sie thun dann
3
3
fz

F
way pre - vail - ing, 'Tis a meth-od nev-er fail-ing. They're half dead with
was wir wol - len, und sie ge - ben, was sie sol - len, bü - cken sich zur
fear. Fra-Bom-barda's men must have their way, In each
Erd! Fra-Bom-bar-da ist's, der com-man-dirt, der zum
fight they win the day. All men lead - ing, Tho' we watch are heeding,
Ruhm und Sieg uns führt! Wir sind Hü - ter doch zugleich Ge-bie-ter,
CHOR
All men lead - ing, Tho' we watch are heeding,
Wir sind Hü - ter doch zugleich Ge-bie-ter,
Guards by night, Yet we hold much pow'r and might. might.
hal - ten Wacht, a - ber hal - ten auch die Macht! Macht!
Guards by night, Yet we hold much pow'r and might. might.
hal - ten Wacht, a - ber hal - ten auch die Macht! Macht!

cresc. al f
F
Ev'-ry burgher rul-ing, We from them per-mit no fooling. 'Tis their humble
Strei-fet durch die Gas-sen, las-set nimmer mit Euch spassen, denn der Bür-ger
Ev'-ry burgher rul-ing, We from them per-mit no fooling. 'Tis their humble
Strei-fet durch die Gas-sen, las-set nimmer mit Euch spassen, denn der Bür-ger
cresc. al f
task, To give us what-so-e'er we ask, We rule with ease these
giebt, was an zu-neh-men uns be-liebt! Wir wis-sen uns Re-
task, To give us what-so-e'er we ask, We rule with ease these
giebt, was an zu-neh-men uns be-liebt! Wir wis-sen uns Re-
stu-pid cat-tle, We do it well, None dare re-bel.
speckt zu schaf-fen, man wagt kein Wort, gehorcht so-fort.
stu-pid cat-tle, We do it well, None dare re-bel.
speckt zu schaf-fen, man wagt kein Wort, gehorcht so-fort.

F
If they pro - test, our swords we rat - tle, And then at
In star - ker Hand führ'n wir die Waf - fen. Ein Blick von
If they pro - test, our swords we rat - tle, And then at
In star - ker Hand führ'n wir die Waf - fen. Ein Blick von
fz
F
once they're dumb be-neath our thumb, And then at once they're dumb
uns ge - nügt, dass man sich fügt, ein Blick von uns ge - nügt,
once they're dumb be-neath our thumb, And then at once they're dumb
uns ge - nügt, dass man sich fügt, ein Blick von uns ge - nügt,
3
fz
F
be-neath our thumb.
dass man sich fügt!
be-neath our thumb.
dass man sich fügt!
3
ff
3
tr
tr
fz

No. 2½. EXIT OF GUARDSMEN.

F
ease these stu - pid cat - tle, We know it well, None dare re - bel,
uns Re - speckt zu schaf - fen, mann wagt kein Wort gehorcht so - fort.
ease these stu - pid cat - tle, We know it well, None dare re - bel.
uns Re - speckt zu schaf - fen, mann wagt kein Wort gehorcht so - fort.
If they pro-test, Our swords we rat - tle, And then at once they're dumb beneath our
In star-ker Hand führ'n wir die Waf - fen. Ein Blick von uns ge - nügt dass man sich
If they pro-test, Our swords we rat - tle, And then at once they're dumb beneath our
In star-ker Hand führ'n wir die Waf - fen. Ein Blick von uns ge - nügt dass man sich
dim. poco a poco.
F
thumb, And then at once they're dumb beneath our thumb.
fügt, ein Blick von uns ge - nügt dass man sich fügt!
thumb, And then at once they're dumb beneath our thumb.
fügt, ein Blick von uns ge - nügt dass man sich fügt!
p
decresc.
tr
pp

6173 + 191

Nº 3. Duett.

Allegretto.
SPARACANI.
CASTRUCCI.
Allegretto. ♩ = 112.
PIANO.
f
p
Fath - er now, and Son - in - law,
Schwieger - va - ter, Schwiegersohn,
That is set - tled quite. 'Tis a bar - gain with - out flaw, Eve - ry thing's all
das ist ab - ge - macht! Al - les ist in Ord - nung schon, Al - les ist be -
right.
dacht.
What Cas - truc - ci says to you, That is al - ways true.
Was Cas - truc - ci Euch verspricht, da - ran zwei - felt nicht!

rit.
a tempo.
27
I am fill'd with great de-light, I can trust him quite. Fath-er now, and
Spa-ro-ca-nis Le-bensglück krönt der Au-gen-blick! Schwieger-va-ter,
rit.
f a tempo.
Son-in-law, That is set-tled quite.... In the bar-gain not a flaw,
Schwiegersohn, das ist ab-ge-macht!.. Al-les ist in Ordnung schon,
Eve-rything's all right. But the maid has not consented, Will she for me
Al-les ist be-dacht! Doch, was wird die Hol-de sa-gen, die ich hoch-ver-
care?
eh'r?
rit. a tempo.
On that matter be contented, I am master there.
Ei, die wer-den wir nicht fra-gen, zweifelt drum nicht mehr!
rit.
f a tempo.

S
C
Fath - er now, and Son - in - law, All is set - tled quite. . . . . .
Schwieger - va - ter, Schwie - gersohn, das ist ab - ge - macht! . . . . .
cres.
In the bond there's not a flaw, There's not a flaw, There's not a flaw, In the bond there's
Al - les ist in Ord - nung schon, in Ord - nung schon, in Ord - nung schon; Al - les ist in
not a flaw, Eve - ry - thing's all right.
Ord - nung schon, Al - les ist be - dacht!
rit.
Moderato.
CASTRUCCI.
Of Wolf, of Mar - tin, Lynx and
Von Wolf, vom Il - tis, Mar - der,

S
Of Wolf, of Mar_tin, Lynx and cat,
Vom Wolf, vom Il_tis, Mar_der, Luchs,
C
cat, Of Sa_ble, Ot_ter, and of
Luchs, vom Zo_bel, Her_me_lin und
S
Of Sa_ble, Ot_ter, and of Rat,
vom Zo_bel, Her_me_lin und Fuchs,
C
rat, Of Mon_key, Fox, and Po_lar
Fuchs, vom Af_fen, Ha_sen, Büf_fel
S
Of Monkey, Fox and Polar Bear,
vom Affen, Hasen, Büffel Bär
Of the tim_id Hare;
und dergleichen mehr
C
Bear, Of wild Hy_e_na, tim_id Hare, In
Bär vom Vielfrass und der_gleichen mehr, von
Allegretto.
S
And
Und
C
fact, of hide of ev'_ry cur, I can dress up the fur.
Allen gerbt ich Fel_le schon, das Gerben lieb, ich sehr!
Allegretto.

30
I shall be his Son-in-law. What pride my heart will stir. And I shall be his
ich, ich bin der Schwiegersohn, das ist mir ei-ne Ehr! und ich, ich bin der
What pride his heart will stir.
das ist mir ei-ne Ehr!
Son-in-law, What pride my heart will stir. Each
Schwiegersohn, das ist mir ei-ne Ehr! Jed-
What pride his heart will stir.
Das ist mir ei-ne Ehr!
Moderato.
an-i-mal with skin and hair, We can fix up with beauty
we-des ed-le Säugethier, das heissen wir willkommen
Each an-i-mal with skin and hair,
Jedwedes ed-le Säugethier,
Moderato.
rare, But moths and insects of that kind, An
hier, nur der Insek-ten läs-tig Heer, das
We can fix up with beauty rare.
das heissen wir willkommen hier,
But moths and insects of that kind,
nur der Insekten lästig Heer

S: awful injury we find, And when them in a skin I
ist für Pelze ein Malheur. Drum sind die Motten mir ein

C: Those we hateful find,
Das ist ein Malheur!

Allegretto.

S: see, I beat them till they flee. But I shall be his
Graus, ich klopf' sie alle aus! Doch ich, ich bin der

Allegretto.

S: Son-in-law, And he will not beat me, But I shall be his
Schwiegersohn, mich klopfet Ihr nicht aus, doch ich, ich bin der

C: And you shall welcome be,
Euch öffne ich das Haus!

S: Son-in-law, And he will not beat me.
Schwiegersohn, mich klopfet Ihr nicht aus!

C: But you shall welcome be.
Euch öffne ich das Haus!

Nº 3 a. Melodram.

Nº 3b Lied.

Andante.
RITA.
Andante. ♩= 72.
espress. e cres.
PIANO.
pp
dim.
p
1. Soon has van_ished all the sing _ ing,
2. In my heart a hope is swell _ ing,
1. Gleich ver_schwom_men fer _ nen Sän _ gen,
2. In des ban_gen Her_zens Tie _ fen,
All the songs have swift_ly flown, On_ly in my heart is ring _ ing
Spite of rea_son's som_bre frown, And it will not leave its dwell _ ing;
wogt um mich der Glo_cken Schall, lei_se zit_tert noch im Her _ zen,
still ver_borg_ne Hoff_nung keimt; Hoff_nung, die wie Mor_gen_glü _ hen,
Still the ech_o of their tone. I to Heav'n would now be pray _ ing;
Ev_ery doubt with light 'twill crown, Hope can bloom 'mid ev_ery per _ il,
frommer Lie_der Wie_der_hall! Fle_hen wollt' ich dort zum Him _ mel
Ne_bel_wol_ken ro_sig säumt! Hoff_nung sprosst als zar_te Blü _ the
Dark and troubled is the hour, Sor_row is my bos_om sway _ ing,
It can laugh at sor_row's power, Ev_en in a soil most ster _ ile,
weil mein Herz be_kümmert schwer wollt' die ir_di_schen Ge_dan _ ken
auch auf Fel_sen, starr und kahl; Hoffnung lä_chelt un_ter Thrä _ nen,

34
R
I would seek re - lig - ion's pow'r,
It will blos - som as a flow'r,
sen - ken in der Andacht Meer!
blinkt wie fer - nen Ster - nes Strahl,
But a - las e'en this was fail - ing,
Hope still paints the fu - ture glow - ing,
Doch ich ar - me Wahn - be - thör - te,
Hoff - nung ist auch mir ge - blie - ben
8
loco
f
dim.
rit.
Eve - ry pi - ous wish grew dim,
Says that fate may not be grim,
kann dem Zau - ber nicht ent - fliehn:
drum ge - lobt ich stark und kühn:
con amore.
All my pray'rs were un - a - vail - ing,
Says that for - tune kinder grow - ing,
Sei - ne Stim - me nur ich hör - te,
Ihm zu glau - ben ihn, zu lie - ben,
rit.
mf
For I on - ly thought of him.
Yet may bring me near to him.
dachte im - mer nur an ihn!
und zu hoffen nur auf ihn!
All my pray'rs were un - a - vail - ing,
Says that for - tune kinder grow - ing,
Sei - ne Stim - me nur ich hör - te,
Ihm zu glau - ben, ihn zu lie - ben,
1.
For I on - ly thought of him.
dachte im - mer nur an ihn!
p
pp
2.
f
pp
2. Yet may bring me near to him, to him, to him!
2. Und zu hoffen nur auf ihn! Auf ihn! Auf ihn!
trem.
espress.
p
pp
f

Nº 4. Duett.
35
Allegretto.
RITA.
ANGELO.
PIANO.
You? What you are near me!
Du in meiner Nähe!
Not quite a - lone!
Nicht ganz al - lein!
Ah what joy and
Lang entbehrtes
bliss. Yet 'tis rash I fear me.
Glück! Doch wenn man dich sä - he!
con amore.
What - ev - er
Was unserm
sor - row fate may have in store for me, To you will cling my heart, And will not
Her - zens - kun - de mag ent - ge - gen stehn, du bleibst al - lein mein Glück, dich lieb' ich
parted be. Oh un - ex - pect - ed joy. Since you a - gain I see; Yet danger
immer - dar! O, welch' Ent - zü - cken bringt mir die - ses Wie - der - sehn, doch wirst ent -
- threatens here, more cautious be, Yes, more cautious be, oh more cautious be.
deckt du hier, droht uns Ge - fahr, ja, uns droht Ge - fahr, ach uns droht Ge - fahr!

36
Più mosso.
R
For ren_dez_vous, my dearest friend; Far too much risk is here; A spy may
Zum Stelldich_ein, ge_lieb_ter Freund gefährlich ist der Ort! Ein Spä_her
pp
all our pleasures end, And danger great I fear.
all zu bald er scheint, drum eile wieder fort!
ANGELO.
p
What e'er my fate, I'll here re_main, Your
Was mir auch droht, ich bleibe hier, zu
A
loving face to see; To part now, were too great a pain, So do not go from
lauschen dei_nem Wort. Es scheidet Licht und Leben mir eilst du Ge_lieb_te
me.
fort.
RITA.
Tho' bit_ter fate may bid us part, I nev_er, love, will forget
Wie bit_ter auch der Trennung Pein, dein Bild ist im_mer mir nah.
fz
p
That you a_lone ruled o'er my heart, From that first hour we met.
Seit je_ner Stunde bin ich dein, da ich zuerst dich sah!
f
fz

37
Moderato. ♩= 100.
ANGELO.
I too, still think On that hour
Nach denk' ich stets der süs - sen
fz
p
beam - ing, When in the wood - land First we did meet. In both our
Stun - de, als ich im Hai - ne ein - sam dich fand; da mir dein
cres.
hearts Woke ten - der dream - ing, And in our bosoms, love ech - oed
Blick gab Himmels - kun - de, da dein Er - röthen mir Lieb' ge -
Poco più mosso.
RITA
sweet. The words you spoke Were full of feeling, And I could not their pow - er withstand,
stand! Dem Liebesfleh'n zu wiederstreben, vermocht ich nicht, ich reicht' dir die Hand.
f
rit.
On both of us Love's light was stealing, To you I gave my hand.
Wir sind vereint für's ganze Leben, geschlossen ist das Band
Yes, to me you gave your
Ja ge - schlossen ist das
dim.
6173—191

38
Allegretto.
hand! No hour of change since then my heart has known, It
Band! Für dich, für dich schlägt die ses Herz al - lein, seit
rit.
Allegretto. ♩= 52.
beats and lives for you,and you a - lone. And there was one who
ich dich fand im stillen dunkeln Hain. Den Schwur der Treu; nicht
RITA.
heard your vows to me, A wit - ness still, yet present there was he. Who
Hört' ich ihn al - lein; ein Zeu - ge, war noch in dem stillen Hain. Im
ANGELO.
Ah yes, 'Twas he. And in the woods were three, And
Im Hain! Im Hain! Wir wa - ren dort zu drei'n, wir
ran it be? And in the woods were three, And
Hain? Im Hain? Wir wa - ren dort zu drei'n, wir
pp trem.
Più
riten.
Ped.
rall.
in the woods were three, And in the woods were three.
wa - ren dort zu drei'n, im stil - len dun - keln Hain!
ri - ten.
rall.
6173-191 Ped.

Moderato.
R
Yes, for Cu_pid lingered near us, While we dal_lied in the wood;
Ja, der Kna_be war's, der Hol_de, der uns dort im Hain ver_band,
p
mf
With a pure de_light did hear us, As he by us laughing stood,
der im blon_den Locken_gol_de, un_ge_se_hen bei uns stand,
mf
With a pure de_light did hear us, As he by us laugh_ing stood.
der im blon_den Lo_cken_gol_de un_ge_se_hen bei uns stand.
f
f
Yes, 'twas Cu_pid lin_gered near us, In the deep and lone_ly wood,
Ja, der Kna_be war's der Hol_de, der uns dort im Hain ver_band,
A
f
Laughing_ly the god did hear us, As his shafts flew where we stood.
der im blon_den Lo_cken_gol_de, un_ge_se_hen bei uns stand,

R
A
rit.
Vivace.
Laughing-ly the god did hear us, As his shafts flew where we stood.
der im blon-den Lo-cken-gol-de un-ge-se-hen bei uns stand.
ff
Tempo di Valse.
pp dolce assai.
Yes, 'twas Cu-pid gave us greet-ing,
Ja, Gott A-mor war zu-ge-gen;
pp
As we through the woods did rove, And our hearts more rap-id beat-ing,
uns ver-ein-te sei-ne Hand. An des Her-zens schnel-len Schlägen
Told us of the birth of love.
hab' ich sei-ne Näh' er kannt.
Animato.
p
All the world seemed full of
Wunder sah ich rings er
6173—181

R
A
Nev - er seemed the earth so bright.
Ach, wie war die Welt so schön!
light.
steh'n!
All the world seem'd
Wun der sah ich
m.g.
m.g.
mf cres.
f
dim.
p
Nev - er was the earth so bright,
All a -
Ach, wie war die Welt so schön!
Rings - um
full of light.
rings er - steh'n!
stacc.
decres.
p
f
round in joy was blend - ing, Bliss with in our hearts had stirred,
sah ich's herr - lich blü - hen Al - les strahl - te licht - ver - klärt;
Heav'n's pure har - mo - nies de - scend - ing, By us both en - tranced were
und des Him - mels Har - mo - ni - en ha - ben rau - schen wir ge -

42
heard. Cu_pid hearing all, Stood as wit_ness by; So what_e'er be_fall,
hört. A_mor hat den Bund, hat den Bund geweiht, der uns_ eint, uns eint
Cu_pid hear_ing
A_mor hat den,
Love shall nev_er die. Cu_pid hearing all, Stood as wit_ness by; And what_
ja für al_le Zeit; A_mor hat den Bund, hat den Bund geweight, der uns
Cu_pid hear_ing
A_mor hat den,
e'er be_fall, Our fond love which we vowed, Our fond love it shall nev_er die,
eint, uns eint der uns eint. A_mor hat den Bund für al_le Zeit ge_weiht,
Allegro assai.
Yes, it shall nev_er, nev_er, nev_er die.
ja, ja, für al_le al_le al_le Zeit!
6173—191

Nº 4½. Melodram.

6173 ⊕ 191

Nº 5. Finale.

Allegro con brio.
PIANO
1st. GROUP.
What is up? What means this clat_ter? Fra Bom_bar_da rushes
Sagt, was giebts? Was ist ge_sche_hen? Ei_lig Fra Bom_bar_da
2d. GROUP.
here. What is up? In haste and clat_ter, Fra Bom_bar_da rushes here........
naht. Sagt was giebts? Was ist ge_sche_hen? Ei_lig Fra Bom_bar_da naht........
here........
naht........

3rd. GROUP.

Something weighty is the mat-ter, Trouble
Et-was Neu-es giebts zu se-hen in Be-

4th. GROUP.

Something weighty is the mat-ter, Trouble in the State we fear........
Et-was Neu-es giebts zu se-hen, in Be-sorgniss ist die Stadt.......

in the State we fear..................................
sorgniss ist die Stadt..................................

ALL THE WOMEN.

When the
Wo er

ALL THE MEN.

Here he comes with angry mien, All his hirelings, too, are seen. When the
Mit den Söldnern, die ihm treu, ei-let zornig er her-bei! Wo er

ty_rant so ap - pears, Eve_ry one has cause for fears, Yes, for fears.
scheinet der Ty - rann, kündet's nim_mer Gu_tes an. O Ty_rann!
ty_rant so ap - pears, Eve_ry one has cause for fears, Yes, for fears.
scheinet der Ty - rann, kündet's nim_mer Gu_tes an. O Ty_rann!
FEMALE CHORUS.
Still we should be laugh_ing, sing_ing, Since the ty_rant wills it
Da_bei soll man hei_ter la_chen, Fra Bom_bar_da es ge_
so
bot
FULL CHORUS.
Still we must be laughing, singing, For the tyrant wills it so
Da_bei soll man heiter lachen, Fra Bombarda es ge_bot
'T would some punishment be bringing, Did we not good hu_mor
Lasst uns gu_te Mie_ne ma_chen, weil sonst schwere Stra_fe

show ....
droht ....
'Twould some pun_ish_ment be bringing, Did we not good hu_mor show ....
Lässt uns gu_te Mie_ne ma_chen, weil sonst schwe_re Stra_fe droht ....
Fruitless would re_sist_ance be, For with_in his pow'r are
Furcht_los wä_re Wi_der_stand, denn wir sind in sei_ner
.... Fruitless would re_sist_ance be, For with_in his pow'r are
.... Furcht_los wä_re Wi_der_stand, denn wir sind in sei_ner
we Yes, en_tire_ly in his hands, We must do what he com_mands.
Hand. Er re_girt und comman_dirt; was er will wird aus_ge_führt!
we. Yes, en_tire_ly in his hands, We must do what he com_mands.
Hand. Er re_girt und comman_dirt; was er will wird aus_ge_führt!

To a-void all chance of
'S ist das Klügste, oh-ne
To a-void all chance of e-vil, is our wisest course by far
'S ist das Klügste, oh-ne Zweifel, wenn wir ihm Gehorsam weih'n
m.g.
e-vil, Is our wisest course by far.
Zweifel, wenn wir ihm Ge-hor-sam weih'n.
Is our wisest course by far. Though we wish him to the dev-il, We will
wenn wir ihm Ge-hor-sam weih'n. Wünscht auch Je-der ihn zum Teu-fel, lasst uns
Though we wish him to the devil, We will loudly shout hur-rah, We will
Wünscht auch Je-der ihn zum Teufel, lasst uns dennoch Vi-vat schrein, lasst uns
loudly shout hur-rah
dennoch Vi-vat schrei'n
We will loudly shout hur-rah, We will
lasst uns dennoch Vi-vat schrein, lasst uns
m.g.
fz

49
loudly shout hurrah, We will loudly shout "Hur-rah," yes, shout "Hur - rah.".........
dennoch Virat schrein, lasst uns dennoch Vi - vat schrein, ja Vi - vat schrein! .....
loudly shout hurrah, We will loudly shout "Hur-rah," yes, shout "Hur - rah.".........
dennoch Virat schrein, lasst uns dennoch Vi - vat schrein, ja Vi - vat schrein! .....
Allegretto.
6173 ... 131

L'istesso Tempo.
Fra BOMB.
I'm
Der
ALL: Hurrah, Fra Bombarda. Hurrah, Hurrah.
L'istesso Tempo.
Fr. B
sure that each one knows me, And I'm ruler In this town: If a-ny dare op-pose me, I will
Fra Bombarda bin ich, bin Ge-bie-ter In Flo-renz! An An-seh'n stets ge-winn' ich Keiner
PERPETUA col Sopran.
At the repeat. In this town;
In Flo-renz!
FORTEBRACCIO col Ten.
At the repeat.
CHOR.
quickly put them down. I am leader in the ci-ty, I am wis-est in the
wa-git Re-ni-tenz! Ich bin klü-ger hier als Al-le, bin als Herrscher ein Ge-
put them down. in the
Re-ni-tenz! ein Ge-
CHOR

51
Fr
B
state. To my foes I show no pi-ty since I am so ve-ry great. I'm
nie. Bring die Fein-de stets zum Fal-le denn ich ha-be E-ner-gie! Der
state
nie.
ve-ry great
E-ner-gie!
pi-ty since I am so ve-ry great. To those who to us cling We can all fa-vors
Fal-le, denn ich ha-be E-ner-gie! D'rum wer mit uns es hält, mit dem ist's gut be-
ve-ry great
E-ner-gie!
bring Our gold has pleasant ring, And we it free-ly fling. But
stellt, wir ha-ben immer Geld, und uns gehört die Welt. doch
those who don't o-bey and vote the oth-er way, We sure-ly find some means to pay. They
wer uns nicht parirt, und gar nach op-po-nirt, dess Ei-genthum wird confiscirt, dem

52
Fr.
B.
find it far from gay. To those who to us cling We can all fa-vors bring Our
Staatsschatz zuge-führt! Drum wer mit uns es hält, mit dem ist's gut be-stellt wir
ppp
To those who to us cling We can all fa-vors bring. Our
Drum wer mit uns es hält, mit dem ist's gut be-stellt wir
pp
gold has pleasant ring And we it free-ly fling, But those who dont o-bey, and
ha-ben immer Geld, und uns gehört die Welt; doch wer uns nicht pa-rirt und
cres
fz
vote the oth-er way We sure-ly find some means to pay They find it far from gay. Then sing
gar noch op-po-nirt, dess' Ei-genthum wird confiscirt, dem Staatsschatz zu-ge-führt! Darum
f
ff

Fr.
B.
praises to free-dom, To lib-er-ty's shrine, Let Springtime and glad-ness
prei-set die Frei-heit in fro-hem Ver-ein, heut' lacht uns die Lust in
praises to free-dom, To lib-er-ty's shrine, Let Springtime and glad-ness
prei-set die Frei-heit in fro-hem Ver-ein, heut' lacht uns die Lust in
o-ver us shine; Who cares for the sor-row to-mor-row may bring,
son-ni-gem Schein; heut' küm-mert uns nicht was da mor-gen wird sein,
fz
o-ver us shine; Who cares for the sor-row to-mor-row may bring,
son-ni-gem Schein; heut' küm-mert uns nicht was da mor-gen wird sein,
fz
fz
fz
8
tr
fz
This day we'll laugh, and we'll sing, Hurrah then, So sing sing, Hurrah then. I'm
heut' herrscht die Freu-de al-lein! Hurrah hoch! Darum lein! Hurrah hoch! Der
1.
2.
ff
ff
mf
This day we'll laugh, and we'll sing, Hurrah then, So sing sing, Hurrah then.
heut' herrscht die Freu-de al-lein! Hurrah hoch! Darum lein! Hurrah hoch!
ff
ff
ff
p

54
Fr. B.
sure that each one knows me, And I'm ruler In this town. If a-ny dare op-pose me, I will
Fra Bombarda bin ich, bin Ge-bieter In Flo-renz! An Anseh'n stets gewinn' ich, Keiner
In this town.
In Flo-renz!
quickly put them down; I am leader in the city, I am wisest in the state; To my
waget Re-ni-tenz! Ich bin klüger hier als Alle, bin als Herrscher ein Ge-nie! Bring' die
put them down;
Re-ni-tenz!
In the state;
Ein Ge-nie!
cres. assai.
Presto.
foes I show no pity, for I am so very great.
Feinde schnell zu Falle den ich habe E-ner-gie!
very great.
E-ner-gie!
con forza.
6173—191

Fr
B
Moderato ♩ 104
p
grazioso.
The love-ly wo - - men here, to them my
Der hol-den Frau - - en Kranz soll nun be-
thanks I pay, For they make full of light our charming holi-day. The love-ly
grü - sset sein, der un-sern Fe-sten Glanz und Far-be wird ver-leih'n, der hol-den
wo - men here, to them my thanks I pay, For they make full of light our pleasant ho-li-
Frau - en Kranz soll nun be-grü sset sein, der un-sern Fe-sten Glanz und Far-be wird ver-
-day.
leih'n!
Yes, tis with pleas - - ure that I
Ja, mit Ver-gnü - - gen seh' ich
f
see, that I see them gath-er near, yes gath-er ve-ry
sie, seh' ich sie in mei-ner Näh', ja ganz in mei-ner
6173-191

56
SPARACANI.
CASTRUCCI.
near gath-er oh ex-treme-ly near. Oh dear, Oh dear! He
Näh', ganz in mei-ner näch-sten Näh! O weh, o weh! Jetzt
f mg
p
FRA BOMBARDA.
S C
now is com-ing near. my friend pray in-tro-duce me to your
kommt er in die Näh! Herr Schöf-fe, stellt uns doch die Gat-tin
PERPETUA. FRA BOMBARDA. CASTRUCCI.
Fr B
wife, There it be-gins. And to your daughter too the pret-ty Ri-ta, Oh dear you're
vor! Da ha-ben wir's! Auch Eu-er Töch-ter-lein, die hol-de Ri-ta, Ich bitt', ver-
SPARACANI.
C
quite too kind, I'm sure you need not mind. Since you ask She's my
zei-hen Sie, ich bitt', ver-zei-hen Sie Ri-ta ist mei-ne
FRA BOMBARDA.
S
bride What real-ly? Oh dam-na-tion! I
Braut! Wahr-haf-tig? O wie scha-de! Das
f
ff
f
6173-191

ritard. à tempo.

Fr. B.
mean. I give to you Sin-cere con-grat-u-la-tion. Yes 'tis a
heisst, ich gra-tu-lir' und schenk' Euch meine Gna-de! Ja mit Ver-

pleas - ure great to me, That I see Them gath-ered
gnü - gen seh' ich sie, seh' ich sie, in mei - ner

near, yes gath-ered ve-ry near, gath-ered quite ex-treme - ly
Näh', ja ganz in mei-ner Näh', ganz in mei - ner, näch - sten

RITA. Allegro con brio.
Oh dear, Oh dear Now he is get-ting near.
O weh, o weh, jetzt kommt er in die Näh!

PERPETUA.

Fr. B.
near.
Näh!

SPARACANI. CASTRUCCI.
Oh dear, Oh dear Now he is get-ting near.
O weh, o weh, jetzt kommt er in die Näh!

Allegro con brio. ♩=152

R
What is't what can it be What can it be What is't What
Was giebt's, was ist gescheh'n, was. ist gescheh'n! Was giebt's, was

P
Let's see what this may be What can it be What is't What
Lasst seh'n was dort gescheh'n, was. gescheh'n! Was giebt's, was

Fr B
What is't what can it be What is't what can it be Let's see What
Was giebts was ist geschehn Was giebts, was ist geschehn, Was giebt's, was

S C
Let's see what this may be What can it be What is't What
Lasst seh'n, was dort gescheh'n, was gescheh'n! Was giebt's, was

Let's see what
Was giebt's, was

fz

R
can it be Let's see what this may be.
ist gescheh'n? Lasst seh'n! was ist ge - scheh'n?

P

Fr B
this may be let's see Let's see.
ist ge - scheh'n? Lasst seh'n, lasst seh'n!

S C
can it be Let's see what this may be
ist gescheh'n? Lasst seh'n! was ist ge - scheh'n?

fz
this may be let's see, Let's see
ist ge - scheh'n? Lasst sehn, lasst seh'n!

fz

tr

fz

6173-191

R
What is't? What can it be? What can it be? They've caught a
Was giebt's, was ist geschehn, was ist gescheh'n? Ge_fan_gen
P
Fr B
What is't? What can it be? What is't? What can it be? They've caught a
Was giebt's, was ist gescheh'n, was giebt's, was ist geschehn, Ge _ fan _ gen
S C
What is't? What can it be? What can it be? They've caught a
Was giebt's, was ist geschehn, was ist gescheh'n? G. fan_gen
They've caught a
Ge _ fan _ gen
R
spy, 'tis he, He will not soon get free! .... Oh God! What do I
ein Spi_on! Wie wird es dem er_geh'n .... O Gott! Was muss ich
P
Fr B
spy, 'Tis he! .... Let's see.
ein Spi_on! .... Was giebt's?
S C
spy, 'tis he He will not soon get free!.. Let's see.
ein Spi_on! Wie wird es dem er_geh'n?. Was giebt's?
spy, 'tis he, He will not soon get free! ....
ein Spi_on! Wie wird es dem er_geh'n ....
spy, 'Tis he! .... Let's see
ein Spi_on! .... Was giebt's?
ff

60
R
see.
seh'n
FORTEBRACCIO col Tenor.
Tenor.
GUARDS
WACHEN
Yes, the spy we were sur - pris - ing, Ere his
Wir er grif - fen den Ver - rä - ther ja, wir
Bass.
ff
WACHEN.
work was well be - gun, Useless was his cloak dis - guis - ing, Why 'tis Ma - la - not - tis'
brin - gen den Spi - on: Nur hier - her, du Mis - se - thä - ter! Es ist Ma - la - not - tis
ERA BOMBARDA.
f
R
Ma - la - not - tis' son! What has he done?
Ma - la - not - tis Sohn! Er ein Spi - on?
Più lento.
P
Fr. B.
son! What has he done?
Sohn! Er ein Spi - on?
FORTEB.
When
Ver-
S C
Ma - la - not - tis' son! What has he done?
Ma - la - not - tis Sohn! Er ein Spi - on?
CHOR.
Ma - la - not - tis' son! What has he done?
Ma - la - not - tis Sohn! Er ein Spi - on?
ff
fz
p
Più lento.

F

First sur-prise he tried to flee But we would not let him free.
klei-det wollt' er uns ent-flieh'n, a-ber wir er-grif-fen ihn!

p m.g.

ff

PERPETUA.

f

Me-lan-ot-tis son!
Ma-lan-ot-tis' Sohn!

FRA BOMBARDA.

F

f

Yes a spy's work he has done
Ja, hier ist er, der Spi-on!

SPARACANI.

CASTRUCCI.

Me-lan-ot-tis son!
Ma-lan-ot-tis Sohn!

Me-lan-ot-tis son!
Ma-lan-ot-tis Sohn!

m.d.

ff

Andante con moto

S
C

p *f*

He is a spy? Woe to the state? If this be so danger is
Er ein Spion? Ist es denn wahr? So droht Verrath? So naht Ge-

He is a spy? Woe to the state? If this be so danger is
Er ein Spion? Ist es denn wahr? So droht Verrath? So naht Ge-

Andante con moto. ♩=88

f

62
S
C
Larghetto.
great. If this be so Dan-ger is great.
fahr? Er ein Spion? Ist es denn wahr?
ANGELO.
great. If this be so Dan-ger is great.
fahr? Er ein Spion? Ist es denn wahr?
Though dis-guise was
Ob auch wehr - los
Larghetto. ♩ = 72
A
un - a - vail - ing Still my cour - age is not fail-ing. In their wrath I'll
und ge - fan - gen, kenn ich nim - mer Furcht und Bangen; die Ge - fahr von
RITA.
His dis - guise was
Mich er - grei - fen
A
bold - ly meet them, I have means yet to de - feat them. Though dis - guise was
mir zu wen - den hab' ein Mit - tel ich in Hän - den Ob auch wehr - los
FRA BOMB.
His dis - guise was
Der Ver - rä - ther
SPARACANI.
CASTRUCCI.
PERPETUA. col Sopran
His dis-guise was
Der Ver - rä - ther
FORTEBRACCIO. col Ten

R
un_a_vail_ing, Now his fate I am be_wailing, Oh may Heav'n some
Furcht und Ban_gen seh den Theu_ren ich ge_fangen. Mag der Him_mel
A
un_a_vail_ing, Still my cour_age is not failing; Heav'n to me a
und ge_fan_gen, kenn ich nim_mer Furcht und Bangen; die Ge_fahr von
Fr. B.
un_a_vailing, Now his courage Will be failing, We his course will
ist ge_fangen, ihn er_grei_fen Furcht und Bangen. Ja, wir ha_ben
S C
un_a_vailing, Now his courage Will be failing, We his course will
ist ge_fangen, ihn er_grei_fen Furcht und Bangen. Ja, wir ha_ben
R
cres.
res_cue send_ing, All our grief be quick_ly end_ing.
Ret_tung sen_den, die Ge_fahr von ihn zu wen_den!
A
cres.
means is send_ing, Which my dan_ger shall be end_ing.
mir zu wen_den, hab' ein Mit_tel ich in Hän_den!
Fr. B.
cres.
soon be end_ing; Hope no long_er him be_friend_ing.
ihn in Hän_den, Nie_mand kann ihm Ret_tung sen_den!
S C
cres.
soon be end_ing; Hope no long_er him be_friending.
ihn in Hän_den, Nie_mand kann ihm Ret_tung sen_den!
cres.
f
pp

64
Piu mosso.
Fr. B.
ANGELO.
proudly
Answer give now to my question, What wicked mission brought you nigh? Do not
Ant-wort gieb auf mei-ne Fra-gen: Was führ te heimlich dich hie-her? Fraget.
A
ask, but be-lieve, I have nev-er, nev-er been a spy!
nicht, a-ber glaubt, ein Ver-rä-ther bin ich nim-mer-mehr!
R
No, he nev-er dare to tell it, What mission 'twas that brought him nigh.
Nein, er darf es nim-mer sa-gen, was heimlich ihn geführt hie-her?
Fr. B.
ANGELO.
Answer quickly now, and tell us, What wicked mission brought you nigh? Ask me
Unglückseliger wirst du sa-gen, was führte heimlich dich hie-her? Fraget
S C
Answer quickly now, and tell us, What wicked mission brought you nigh?
Unglückseliger wirst du sa-gen, was führte heimlich dich hie-her?
F
A
not, but be-lieve, I could nev-er, nev-er be a spy!
nicht, a-ber glaubt, ein Ver-rä-ther bin ich nim-mer-mehr!
ritard.

65
Tempo I.
R
His disguise was un_a_vail_ing, Now his fate I am bewailing;
Mich er_grei_fen Furcht und Ban_gen seh den Theu_ren ich ge_fangen.
A
Though disguise was un_a_vail_ing, Still my cour_age is not failing;
Obauch wehr_los und ge_fan_gen, kenn ich nim_mer Furcht und Bangen;
Fr. B.
His disguise was un_a_vail_ing, Now his cour_age Will be fail_ing,
Der Ver_rä_ther ist ge_fangen, ihn er_greifen Furcht und Bangen.
S C
CHOR
PER. col Sop.
His disguise was un_a_vail_ing, Now his cour_age Will be fail_ing,
Der Ver_rä_ther ist ge_fangen; ihn er_greifen Furcht und Bangen.
FORTEB. col Tenor
R
Oh may Heav'n some res_cue send_ing, All our woes be quickly end_ing. Could he but
Mag der Him_mel Ret_tung sen_den, die Gefahr von ihm zu wenden! Dürft ich ge.
A
Heav'n to me a means is send_ing, Which my danger shall be end_ing. Could I but
die Ge_fahr von mir zu wen_den, hab' ein Mit_tel ich in Händen! Dürft ich ge.
Fr. B.
We his course will soon be ending, Hope to him no ray is send_ing.
Ja, wir ha_ben ihn in Händen, Niemand kann ihm Rettung sen_den!
S C
We his course will soon be ending, Hope to him no ray is send_ing.
Ja, wir ha_ben ihn in Händen, Niemand kann ihm Rettung sen_den!

R
A
Fr. B.
S. C.
tell, All would be well, A word t would be, And I were
steh'n, was hier ge - scheh'n, ein Wort al - lein könnt' ihn be - mich
p
Yes, he must tell, What here be - fell, What e'er it be.
Er muss gesteh'n! Wir wol-len seh'n! Mag er auch schreih,
Yes, he must tell, What here be - fell, What e'er it be.
Er muss gesteh'n! Wir wol-len seh'n! Mag er auch schreih,
cres. assai e ritard.
free. And yet this word we must con - ceal, Some hope the
freih. Doch hält' dies Wort ich noch zu - rück, ver - trau-end
He'll not go free. Yes, he the truth must now re-veal, Or he our
man sperrt ihn ein! Und das so fort im Augenblick nichts schützet
He'll not go free. Yes, he the truth must now re-veal, Or he our
man sperrt ihn ein! Und das so fort im Augenblick nichts schützet
cres. assai e ritard.

6173 – 191

Mosso. appassionato.
R
fu - ture may re-veal, Though we may feel the ty-rant's might
auf des Zufalls Glück! Ob uns auch droht Ty.-ran - nen Macht,
A
Fr B
wrath shall sure-ly feel He soon shall feel Bom-bar - da's might
ihn vor dem Ge-schick! Weit rei-chet Fra Bom-bar - da's Macht
S C
wrath shall sure-ly feel He soon shall feel Bom-bar da's might
ihn vor dem Ge-schick! Weit rei-chet Fra Bom-bar - da's Macht
Mosso. ♩=108. appassionato.
f
R
We are not yet des-pair - - ing, Still from a-bove Hope
ob wir auch heut' noch za - - gen, der Hoff-nung Stern hoch
A
Fr B
Then he will be des-pair - - ing, Soon in the dun - geon's
Wer Wi-der-stand will wa - - gen, büsst es in Ker - ker's
S C
Then he will be des-pair - ing, Soon in the dun - geon's
Wer Wi-der-stand will wa - - gen, büsst es in Ker - ker's

8173-191

rit. più a più
Lento. pp
sends its light Beam-ing in sor - rows dark night. If he could tell, All would be
o - ben lacht, strahlend er - hellt er die. Nacht! Dürft ich gesteh'n, was hier ge-
star - less night! He'll be in sor - row-ful flight! Yet he must tell What here be-
grau - ser Nacht! D'rum hal-ten treu wir die Wacht! Wir wollen seh'n, wir wollen
star - less night! He'll be in sor - row-ful flight! Yes he must tell
grau - ser Nacht! D'rum hal - ten treu wir die Wacht! Wir wollen seh'n,
Lento.
well, a word twould be and he were free!
scheh'n, könnt' ich be-freit den Theu - ren seh'n!
- fell. Oh he shall see How harsh we'll be!
seh'n, wird den Ver rath er ein - ge - seh'n!
What here be-fell, Oh he shall see How harsh we'll be!
wir wollen seh'n, wird den Ver rath er ein - ge - seh'n!
trem

Moderato con moto.
FRA BOMBARDA.
Con-fess The duke here sent you as his
Ge- steht, dass Ihr des Her-zogs E-mis-
Moderato con moto.
m.d.
ff
p
m.g.
ANGELO.
Oh no A-noth-er came It was not I And I may
Ich nicht! Ein And'rer kam als sol-cher her. Und zwei Ver-
Fr B
spy.
sär!
f
m.d.
p
A
add that trai-tors two are stand-ing near to you.
rä-ther ha-bet Ihr ganz in der Nä-he hier!
Fr B
Then name them if you
So kennt Ihr sie, sagt

Più lento
A
plan, This night they ope the gate, And let the foemen enter.
Plan, dem Herzog Medi-ci die Stadt heut Nacht zu öffnen!
Ich
Fr
B
Treas-on treason treason here.
Ha Verrath, Verrath, Verrath!
SPARACANI
CASTRUCCI.
Treas-on treason treason here.
Ha Verrath, Verrath, Verrath!
Più lento
Moderato.
A
heard it ve-ry clear.
war ganz in der Näh!
FRA BOMB.
Then
Und
S
C
Oh dear, oh dear, oh dear!
O weh, o weh, o weh!
We see he lin-gered near.
Er war in uns'rer Näh!
Moderato.
Allegro.
Fr
B
give the name.
wer? Wer war's CASTRUCCI.

ANGELO. (aside to Rita.) RITA.
Your fa-ther t'was! Oh God!
Dein Va-ter ist's! O Gott!
FRA BOMB.
lie!
spricht!
Then make re-ply!
Thu dei-ne Pflicht!
p
ff
SPARACANI.
ANGELO.
Let's hear what he'll re - ply!
So hört doch was er spricht!
I
Ich
Let's hear what he'll re - ply!
So hört doch was er spricht!
FRA BOMB.
A
will not tell, not I!
nenn den Na - men nicht!
Not ev - en
Auch dann nicht,
If you else must
wenn dir's Ret-tung
ANGELO.
FRA BOMB.

72
RITA.
ANGELO.
Fr
B
lead him! Oh hold and lis - ten, Hear what I say! Si-lence Ri-ta! lead me a-
To-de! Halt ein, halt ein! O hö - - ret mein. Wort! Schweige, Ri-ta! Führt mich
Allegro moderato.
A
-way!
fort!
Vivace giocoso.
Vivace.
(Chorus of flower girls be-hind
the senes.)
Vivace
126.
1 Now
1 Nun
ban - ish ev-ery sor-row, Let each heart be light and gay; And in the bud-ding
fort mit al-len Lei-den, heu-te herrschet Lust und Freud'; und Ju - bel-lust durch-
2 care should come to-morrow, Then at least were glad to - day; Then join in our ar-
2 Hier die duft'gen Blü-then, die wir gern Euch bie-ten an; drum stimmt in un-ser
FRA BOMB.

Fr. B.
flow-er maids be-hold, Of Whit-sun-tide they're singing, And buds and blos-soms
naht der Mädchen Schaar, das Pfingstfest zu ver-künden, und Blumen uns zu
bring-ing, A cus-tom good and old.
winden, wie's im-mer Sit-te war.
The maids be-hold Of
Schon naht die Schaar, das
SPARACANI.
CASTRUCCI.
The maids be-hold Of
Schon naht die Schaar, das
CHOR.
The flow-er maids be-hold Of
Schon naht die Mädchen Schaar, das
ff p
cres.
f

74
(Flower Girls.)
Now ban-ish every sor-row, Let each heart be light and gay; And
Nun fort mit al-len Leiden, heute herrschet Lust und Freud; und
f
in the bud-ding spring Let all re-joice and sing. If care should come tomorrow, Then at
Jubel-lust durchzieht ein jeg-liches Ge-müth. Nehmt hier die duft'gen Blüthen, die wir
8
least en-joy to-day. So join in our ar-ray, And scat-ter flow'rs to-
gern Euch bie-ten an; und stimmt in un-ser Lied mit hei-te-rem Ge-

R
gain is free, And when he leaves his prison's night,
ret_ten kann wenn es ge_lingt ihn zu be_frei'n,
S
C
great de_light, A great de_light; Forgive your en_e_mies to_day, Forgive to_
brin_gen kann, Euch bringen kann drum sollt den Fein_den Ihr ver_zeih'n, ihr sollt ver_
great de_light, Forgive your en_e_mies to_day,
brin_gen kann, drum sollt den Fein_den Ihr ver_zeih'n,
great de_light, A great de_light; Forgive your en_e_mies to_day, Forgive to_
brin_gen kann, Euch bringen kann drum sollt den Fein_den Ihr ver_zeih'n, ihr sollt ver_
8
3
R
My heart will beat in glad de_light. Ah, joy can
dann lacht auch mir der Son_ne Schein! Ach Freu_de
1.
2.
FRA BOMB.
S
C
day. O'er all let mer_cy now have sway, Let mercy sway. Now Whitsun_ sway. But
zeih'n, und je_de Schuld ver_ge_ben sein, ver_geben sein! Das schöne sein! Nur
O'er all let mer_cy now have sway, Let mercy sway. Now Whitsun_ sway.
und je_de Schuld ver_ge_ben sein, ver_geben sein! Das schöne sein!
day. O'er all let mer_cy now have sway, Let mercy sway. Now Whitsun_ sway.
zeih'n, und je_de Schuld ver_ge_ben sein, ver_geben sein! Das schöne sein!
3
3
mf
6173 — 191

76
ANGELO.
No traitor spy in me you see.
Ver_räther bin ich nicht, o nein!
Fr. B.
spies no mer_cy find in me.
dem Ver_rä_ther kein Verzeih'n!
SPARACANI.
CASTRUCCI.
To pris_on let him
Fort in den Ker_ker
To pris_on let him
Fort in den Ker_ker
f
RITA
No
Ver_
Fr. B.
Base spies no mer_cy find in me.
Nur dem Ver_rä_ther kein Ver_zeih'n!
S C
go, No mer_cy to him show.
schnell, fort in den Ker_ker schnell!
go, No mer_cy to him show.
schnell, fort in den Ker_ker schnell!
mf
6178 _ 191

R
trai-tor spy in him you see!
räther ist er nicht o nein!
ff
Now I
Noch muss
A
ff
Yes I
Ich ver-
Fr
B
ff
Then sing
Da - rum
S
C
ff
To prison let him quickly go, quick-ly go. Then sing
Fort in den Kerker schnell hinein, schnell hi-nein! Da - rum
ff
R
hear deep-est sor-row, my heart throbs in woe, And yet but a word and
schwei-gend ich dul-den die qual-vol-le Pein; ver-mag auch ein Wort ihn
A
feel that I need not give up yet to woe, And yet but a word and
la-che das Dro-hen mit Ker-ker und Pein, leicht könn-te ein Wort da
Fr
B
prais-es to free-dom, Let lib-er-ty glow, Which ev-ery de-light on
prei-set die Frei-heit im fro-hen Ver-ein, heut lacht uns die Lust in
S
C
prais-es to free-dom, Let lib-er-ty glow, Which ev-ery de-light on
prei-set die Frei-heit im fro-hen Ver-ein, heut lacht uns die Lust in

78
R
free - ly he'd go. My fa - ther al - so would the trai - tor's fate know.
leicht zu be - frein', den Va - ter würd sonst den Ver - der - ben ich weih'n,
A
free - ly I'd go, Her fa - ther al - so would the trai - tor's fate know.
von mich be - frein, doch nicht ih - ren Va - ter der Ra - che zu weih'n,
Fr
B
us can be - stow. At pres - ent let joy in a hap - py stream flow.
son - ni - gem Schein; heut küm - mert uns nicht, was da mor - gen wird sein,
S
C
us can be - stow. At pres - ent let joy in a hap - py stream flow.
son - ni - gem Schein; heut küm - mert uns nicht, was da mor - gen wird sein,
R
Nev - er, It must not be so No, No, No! Still they ac - cuse him,
weh' mir, das darf ja nicht sein! Nein, nein, nein! Er ist nicht Thä - ter,
A
Nev - er, It must not be so, No, No, No! Still they ac - cuse me,
will ich ver - schwie - gen noch sein, ja noch sein! Bin nicht der Thä - ter,
Fr
B
Give to the mor - row no thought No, No, No! Yet we'll ac - cuse him,
heut' herrscht der Freu - de al - lein! Hur - rah, hoch! Weh dir, Ver - rä - ther,
S
C
Give to the mor - row no thought No, No, No! Yet we'll ac - cuse him,
heut' herrscht der Freu - de al - lein! Hur - rah, hoch! Weh dir, Ver - rä - ther,
ff

R
Mer - cy refuse him, The traitor he knows him, Yet will not expose him.
auch kein Ver_rä_ther; er tro_tzet der Ra_che, verschweiget die Sa_che.
A
Mer - cy refuse me, The traitor I know him, Yet I will not show him.
auch kein Ver_rä_ther. Nicht fürcht' ich die Ra_che, der Drohung ich la_che!
Fr B
Mer - cy refuse him, In prison enclose him, As spy each one knows him.
Schmach trifft den Thäter! Schon na_het die Ra_che, treu hal_ten wir Wa_che!
S C
Mer - cy refuse him, In prison enclose him, As spy each one knows him.
Schmach trifft den Thäter! Schon na_het die Ra_che, treu hal_ten wir Wa_che!
Prestissimo.
R
Still they accuse him, And grace refuse him, While he scorn doth show. Tho' the
Er ist nicht Thäter, auch kein Verräther, doch er hält Euch Stand! Oh in
A
Still they accuse me, Mer - cy refuse me, Yet my scorn I'll show. Tho' the
Bin kein Verräther, doch ist der Thäter mir gar wohl be_kannt! Oh in
Fr B
Yes we accuse him, Mer - cy refuse him, Let him tor_ture know. Now to
Weh dir Verräther, Schmach trifft den Thäter, der in uns_rer Hand! Zu ge_
S C
Yes we accuse him, Mer - cy refuse him, Let him tor_ture know. Now to
Weh dir Verräther, Schmach trifft den Thäter, der in uns_rer Hand! Zu ge_
fz
Prestis - simo.
6173 — 131

80
R
tyrant, hate is showing, As his glances on him bend, Heav'n will yet be mer-cy
Fra Bombarda's Zügen grausam Hohn und Tücke glimmt, bald wird es der Him-mel
A
tyrant, hate is showing, As his glances on me bend, Heav'n will yet be mer-cy
Fra Bombarda's Zügen grausam Hohn und Tücke glimmt, bald wird es der Him-mel
Fr
B
pleasure without measure, Let each one in rapture bend, 'Tis a hol-i-day we
niessen das Ver-gnügen, eh' der Freude Rausch verglimmt, schlürft die Lust in vol-len
S
C
pleasure without measure, Let each one in rapture bend, 'Tis a hol-i-day we
niessen das Ver-gnügen, eh' der Freude Rausch verglimmt, schlürft die Lust in vol-len
R
showing, And his pow'r find sud-den end. Tho' the sud-den end, A
fü-gen, dass die Macht ein En-de nimmt. Ob in En-de nimmt, ein
A
showing, And his pow'r find sud-den end. Tho' the sud-den end, A
fü-gen, dass die Macht ein En-de nimmt. Ob in En-de nimmt, ein
Fr
B
treasure, Let's en-joy it to the end. Now to ve-ry end, Yes
Zü-gen, bis die Sach' ein En-de nimmt. Zu ge- En-de nimmt, ein
C
treasure, Let's en-joy it to the end. Now to ve-ry end, Yes
Zü-gen, bis die Sach' ein En-de nimmt. Zu ge- En-de nimmt, ein

R
sud - den end. Yes his pow'r find sudden end find sud-den end. Yes his pow'r find sudden
En - de nimmt; dass die Macht ein Ende nimmt ein En - de nimmt; das die Macht ein En-de

A

Fr
B
to the end. Let's en-joy it to the end yes to the end. Let's en-joy it to the
En - de nimmt; bis die Sache ein Ende nimmt ein En - de nimmt; bis die Sach ein En-de

S
C

to the end. Let's en-joy it to the end yes to the end. Let's en-joy it to the
En - de nimmt; bis die Sache ein Ende nimmt ein En - de nimmt; bis die Sach ein En-de

loco.

R
end.
nimmt!

A

Fr
B
end.
nimmt!

S
C

end.
nimmt!

Ende des I. Actes.

II. ACT.

Entr' acte.

ffz
ffz
ff con forza.
fz
fz
fz
fz
ff
pp
dim.
morendo.
ppp
6173 — 191

Nº 6. Bacchanale.

Allegro con fuoco.
85
Fr. B
takes his drink in sol - i - tude, Can - not be in good mood; All the pleasure goes to
if 'tis poured by some fair lass, The deuce is in the glass, Then one at the host - ess
Allegro con fuoco. ♩ = 138.
mf
fz
waste, His wine like med - i - cine must taste; He is not gay while quenching thirst, His
winks, With eve - ry sip he gai - ly drinks, And af - ter each he takes a kiss, Oh
ff
mf
ease is of the worst. If I have friends to drink with me, Then every glass is full of
dear, that's sol - id bliss. Yes if the wine tastes di - vine, Let me have near a sweetheart
fz
glee, A - lone one can - not quench his thirst, The wine seems of the worst; But if good
fine. With eve - ry sip he takes a kiss, Oh dear, that's sol - id bliss. Yes if the
ff

Fr.
B
friends drink with me, Then eve-ry glass is full of glee.
wine tastes di - vine, Let us have near a sweet-heart fine.
Wein soll er - freu'n, la - det mir al - le Freun - de ein!
Wein mun - den fein, la - det mir hüb - sche Mäd - chen ein!
friends drink with me, Then eve-ry glass is full of glee.
wine tastes di - vine, Let us have near a sweet-heart fine.
Wein soll er - freu'n, la - det mir al - le Freun - de ein!
Wein mun - den fein, la - det mir hüb - sche Mäd - chen ein!
ff
Tempo I.
ff
ff

Nº 6½ Exit.

6173 — 191

Fr. B
ff
glee. Who is not gay while quenching thirst. His ease is of the worst; If I have
ein! Der schönste Durst stirbt un-genützt, so-bald man ein-sam sitzt; wenn mich der
ff
ff
Who is not gay while quenching thirst. His ease is of the worst; If I have
Der schönste Durst stirbt un-genützt, so-bald man ein-sam sitzt; wenn mich der
ff
ff
fz
Fr. B
friends drink with me, Then every glass is full of glee.
Wein soll er-freu'n, ladet mir al-le Freunde ein!
friends drink with me, Then every glass is full of glee.
Wein soll er-freu'n, ladet mir al-le Freunde ein!
ff

6173 — 191

Nº 7. Ensemble.

S
C
Here some great subject is de - bat - - ing!
Wich-tiges giebt's zu ü-ber - le - - gen!
Something's wrong.
Was es sei,
Come a-lone,
Was es sei,
Now be prudent.
lasst uns prüfen!
Poco piu mosso.
(very soft)
For development's we're waiting.
lasst uns prüfen und erwägen!
Have a care. Let's give ear,
Ha-bet Acht, spitzt das Ohr!
Something new goes on here.
Grosses geht heut' hier vor
Cautions be. Let us op-po-
Wer sich rührt,
STADTRÄTHE.
Have a care.
Habet Acht,
Now give ear, Something great goes on here. Cautions be.
spitzt das Ohr! Grosses geht heut' hier vor Wer sich rührt,
fz
pp
Poco piu mosso. ♩=112.

S
C
see, In this moment of suspense, Let us sit up.on the fence. If they
nirt wird vom Am.te suspendirt oh.ne Weit'.res pen.sionirt. Wenn um
Let us.see, In this moment of suspense, Let us sit up.on the fence.
op.po.nirt wird vom Amte suspendirt oh.ne Weit'res pensionirt.
ask So or so, Answer "yes," Never "no," Answer
Rath man Euch fragt, sagt nur "Ja" unver.sagt! Immer
If they ask So or so, Answer "yes," Nev.er. "no,"
Wenn um Rath man Euch fragt, sagt nur "Ja" un.ver.sagt!
"yes," Nev.er "no," Such an answer you will see, Safe will be.
"Ja" niemals "Nein" soll im Rathe all.gemein Losung sein!
Answer "yes," Nev.er "no," Such an answer you will see, Safe will be.
Immer "Ja" niemals "Nein" soll im Rathe allgemein Losung sein!

92
From all plots and re-volts now be stay - ing, — Now be stay - ing, — Now be
Plagt Euch nicht mit Protest und Scan-da - len, — mit Scan-da - len, — mit Scan-
stay - ing, — For some trick one is sure to be play - ing, — For some
da - len, — fügt Euch still und macht kei - ne Ka - ba - len, — kei - ne

pay - ing, — Al - ways pay - ing, — Al - ways pay - ing. — They'll as -
zah - len, — im - mer zah - len, — nichts als zah - len! — Gebt nur
sess, and as - sess, While the funds grow less, — While the mon - ey grows less; They'll as -
her, gebt nur her, bis die Taschen leer, — bis die Taschen ganz leer, gebt nur
sess, and as - sess. Yes, the bill you'll be paying.
her, gebt nur her! Schliesslich müsst Ihr doch zahlen!
But be still, For he'll do what he
Schweiget still! Er thut doch was er

94
(very soft)
pp
Have a care, Let's give ear, Something strange, Goes on
Habet Acht, spitzt das Ohr! Grosses geht heut' hier
will.
will!
(very soft.)
Have a care, Let's give ear, Something strange,
Ha-bet Acht, spitzt das Ohr! Gro-sses geht
pp
here; Cautious be, Let us see, In this moment of suspense, Let us
vor. Wer sich rührt, op-po-nirt, wird vom Am-te suspendirt, oh-ne
Goes on here; Cautious be, Let us see, In this moment of suspense,
heut' hier vor. Wer sich rührt, op-po-nirt, wird vom Am-te suspendirt,
keep up-on the fence. If they ask So and so, Answer "yes," Never
Weitres pen-sionirt. Wenn um Rath man Euch fragt, sagt nur "Ja" unver
Let us keep upon the fence. If they ask So and so, Answer "yes,"
oh-ne Weitres pensionirt. Wenn um Rath man Euch fragt, sagt nur "Ja"

S
C
"no" Always "yes," Never "no," Such an answer you will see, Safe will
zagt! Immer "Ja," niemals "Nein" soll im Rathe all - gemein Losung
nev-er "no," Always "yes," Nev-er "no," Such an answer you will see, safe will
un-ver-zagt! Immer "Ja," niemals "Nein" soll im Rathe allgemein Losung
pp
be, Safe will be, He will do,
sein! Seid nur still! Er thut doch,
Yes be still, He will
Seid nur still! Er thut
be,
sein!
a tempo.
p
rit.
pp
ppp rit.
as he will. He will do, as he will. So be still!
was er will! Still und sacht, mit Be-dacht! Seid nur still!
do, as he will.
doch, was er will!
ppp
So be still!
Seid nur still!
rit. ppp
fz
pp
ffz

96
No 8. Spur Song.
Andante con moto.
FRA BOMBARDA
CHOR.
Tenori.
Bassi.
PIANO.
Andante con moto. ♩ = 88.
1. If you
1. Wenn man
follow my commanding, I will never be severe. We shall
ladies, soft and tender, Sweet and gentle, timid. shy; They have
thut, was ich befehle, meinem Winke folgt geschwind, bin ich
Frauen, ach die Frauen, sanft und schüchtern von Natur, zeigen
reach an understanding, Smooth and pleasant, never fear. I'm the
claws like all their gender, But to show them seldom try, No they
eine gute Seele, bleibe huldvoll, wohlgesinnt. Wenn mein
anfangs keine Klauen, wollen schmachten, lieben nur! Ach die
most delightful being, When all others me obey; I'm with
never deal in snarling. Rather will they softly speak: "Do just
Wille wird vollzogen, kann ich recht gemüthlich sein, Allen
lieben süssen Kätzchen geben ja, in Allem nach: "Ganz wie

Fr
B
eve - ry one a - greeing, When they let me have my way; But with
as you wish, my dar - ling," Then the men get ver - y meek. But with
bleib' ich wohl ge - wo - gen, die so mei - nen, wie ich's mein! A - ber
du es wünscht mein Schätzchen!" Und die Män - ner wer - den schwach! Doch weh
8
fz
those who dis - a - gree, I nev - er can so friend - ly be. Yes, when
those who dis - a - gree, They will not so friend - ly be. You may
wer da murrt, mit dem werd' ich leicht un - an - ge - nehm! Op - po -
dem, der wi - der - spricht, ü - ber - zeu - gen giebt es nicht. Je - des
f
rit.
peo - ple cross my mood, They nev - er find me quite so good.'
ar - gue by the hour, But all your words will have no pow'r.
nirt man mir, so - fort ver - leih' ich Nachdruck mei - nem Wort.
Wort. ist da ver - lo - ren, und man pre - digt tau - ben Ohr'n.
f
p rit.
Poco più lento.
p
For my foes to reas - on bring - ing, I've a means at hand:
Ev - en them to reas - on bring - ing, I've my means at hand:
Um den Wi - der - spruch zu kir - ren, hab' ein Mit - tel ich:
Um den Re - de - fluss zu bre - chen, hab' ein Mit - tel ich:
mf
Tempo di Marcia
On - ly let my spurs go ring - ing, Then they un - der - stand.
On - ly let my spurs go ring - ing, Then they un - der - stand.
Lass' ich mei - ne Spo - ren klir - ren, dann ver - steht man mich.
Lass' ich mei - ne Spo - ren spre - chen, dann ver - steht man mich.
mf
f

Fr
B
Ringing sternly, ringing, Ringing, All the foes to rea - son bringing;
Klirret Sporen, klirret, klirrt, schwirret Rädchen schwirret, schwirret!
f
Ringing sternly, Ringing, Ringing, All the foes to rea - son bringing.
Klirret Sporen, klirret, klirret, höret meine Sporen klirren!
f
ff
Such a tread, Must give me sway,
Solch ein Schritt der im - po - nirt,
f
Such a tread, Must give him sway,
Solch ein Schritt der im - po - nirt
All have dread, And must give way, All are
And must o - bey,
nur ein Tritt und man pa - rirt! Al-les
p
pp
m.d.

Fr
B
dumb, All are still, No one dare cross my will. All are dumb,
stumm, Alles still; Jeder weiss, was ich will. Alles stumm
pp
dumb, still, dumb, still. All are dumb
Stumm still, stumm, still; Alles stumm
m.d.
m.g.
Ped.
(Stamps.)
ff
All are still, No one dare cross my will.
Alles still, Jeder weiss, was er will!
All are still, No one dare cross my will.
Alles still, Jeder weiss, was er will!
pp
tenuto.
acceler.
1.
2.
p
2. And the
2. Und die

Nº 8½ Exit.

Andante
FRA BOMBARDA
CHOR. Tenori.
Bassi.
Andante. ♩. = 80.
PIANO.
For my foes to rea_son bringing, I've a means at
Um den Wi_der_spruch zu kir_ren, hab' ein Mit_tel
hand: On_ly let my spurs go ringing, Then they un_der_stand.
ich: Lass'ich meine Spo_ren klirren, dann ver_steht man mich.
Tempo di
Marcia.
Ringing sternly, firmly ringing, All my foes to rea_son bringing,
Klirret Spo_ren klirret, klirret, schwirret Rädchen, schwirret, schwirret!
Ringing sternly, firmly ringing, All my foes to rea_son bringing.
Klirret Spo_ren klirret, klirret, hö_ren mei_ne Spo_ren klir_ren!
6177.191

Fr.
B
Such a stamp
Must give me sway,
All have
Such a tread
Must give him sway.
Solch ein Schritt
dread,
And must give way!
All are dumb,
All are still,
No one dare cross my
Tritt
dumb,
still,
dumb.
(stamp)
(Tritt)
will,
All are dumb,
All are still,
No one dare cross my will!
Al-les stumm,
Al-les still,
Je-der weiss,
was ich will!
still.
All are dumb,
All are still,
No one dare cross his will!
tenuto.
Ped.
m.g.

№9. DUETT.

Allegro.
ANGELO.
CASTRUCCI.
Allegro. ♩.=100.
PIANO.
I know how he's
Ich kenn' sei - ne
Quite bad I am
Verwünscht ist die
feel-ing, One word I'm re - veal - ing, To jail then he'd go, To
La - ge, ein Wört - chen ich sa - ge, so sperrt man ihn ein, so
feel-ing, Should he be re - veal - ing The plot that I know:
La-ge, die kitz - li - che Fra - ge, sie macht mir viel Pein,
jail he would go. It seems that he knows it, His whole man - ner
sperrt man ihn ein. Das scheint er zu - wis - sen, denn ach, sein Ge -
I fear it is so, I cer - tain - ly know it, Yet dread that I
sie macht mir viel Pein. Er scheint was zu wis - sen, und ach, mein Ge -
shows it, His doubts stronger grow, His doubts stron-ger grow,
wis - sen ist lei - der nicht rein, ist lei - der nicht rein,
show it; My doubts stronger grow, My doubts stron-ger grow, My
wis - sen ist lei - der nicht rein, ist lei - der nicht rein, ist

His doubts stronger grow, His doubts stronger grow,
Well
ist lei - der nicht rein, ist lei - der nicht rein!
So
doubts stronger grow,
My doubts stronger grow,
lei - der nicht rein,
ist lei - der nicht rein!
L'istesso Tempo.
Moderato.
CASTRUCCI.
(hesitating)
fire a-way, What do you say?
'Tis hard but
schiesst den los, ich bin ge - fasst!
Zu streng find
Moderato. ♩=80.
(shows the paper.)
then I must o - bey, It fair-ly takes a - way my breath, You see the sentence
ich das Urtheil fast; doch Fra Bom - bar - da so gebot; seht her, das Urtheil
ANGELO.
CASTRUCCI.
here is, Death, Yes but not right a - way, Tomorrow!
lau-tet Tod Tod allerdings; je - doch erst morgen!
ANGELO.
It seems too bad, No need of sor - row.
Mir ist's sehr leid Macht Euch nicht Sor - gen!

104
CASTRUCCI. (puzzled.)
And have they sen-tenced on-ly me? Why yes, who else?
Und trifft das Ur-theil mich al-lein? Ja, wen den noch?
ANGELO (pointedly.)
CASTRUCCI.
Why it could be, that Some oth-ers too were con-spir-ing! By
Es könn-te, sein, dass am Mit-schul-di-ge zu fas-sen des-
(quickly.)
tor-ture they would be inquir-ing, But I'll not let you come to harm, You
halb soll ich Euch fol-tern las-sen, doch thu' ich's nicht, o nein, o nein! Ihr
may re-main quite calm, I will for-bid it, so be calm.
könnt' ganz ru-hig sein, ich thu' es nicht, ich thu' es nicht!
ANGELO. (smiling)
ad lib.
p No, 'tis not need-ed, I, I am quite
Ist auch nicht nö-thig! Ich ich bin ja
pp rit.
p a tempo.

(earnestly.)
ready to confess them, I know a
zu gesteh'n es bis-tig! Ich weiss, wer
fz (frightened.)
Oh!
Oh!
fz p
p
(with meaning.)
traitor very great, They'll
den Verräth ersann! Viel-
(anxiously.)
How?
Wie?
ff
fz
trem.
string. e cresc.
(increasing.)
pardon me when him I state, I'd better speak ere 'tis too
leicht begnadigt man mich dann? Viel-leicht, dass mich das ret-ten
(gasping.)
No!
Nie!
string. e cresc.
m.g.
(softly again.) ad lib.
late, For me 'twill pity waken,
kann? Die Sache scheint doch wich-tig!
(eagerly.) (eagerly.)
Ah!
Nein!
Oh, no you are mistaken; For
Nein, nein, das ist nicht rich-tig; denn
fz
p rit.

Allegretto quasi Andante. ♩=100.
Fra Bom-bar-ba won't be stirred, He will not thus for-
Fra Bom-bar-da, der Ty-rann, lässt da-rauf sich nicht
give, Its no use ut-ter-ing a word, He will not let you
ein; er denkt nicht dran, er denkt nicht dran, er denkt nicht an Ver-
ANGELO. rit.
Vivo. ♩ 160.
(gradually louder.)
live, And yet the thing might be, ___ If I should make it
zeih'n. Es könn-te doch wohl sein! ___ Denn wenn er nun er-
clear, That when the spy came here, ___ That he brought a mes-sage
führt, aus mei-nem Mun-de hört, ___ dass des Her-zogs E-mis-
CASTRUCCI.
rit.
(spoken.)
too, And gave it un-to you, Be si-lent! For vengeance you're
sär zu Euch nur kam hier-her Schweigt stille! Wollt Ihr mich ver-

Andante.
ANGELO. (earnestly.)
try-ing. Oh no! But now for you I'm dy-ing, When by be-tray-ing you I'd
der-ben? Das nicht! Doch soll ich für Euch ster-ben, so will ich wis-sen auch wo-
p
Allegro molto moderato.
live. I mean, what will you give?
für? Ich mein', Was bie-tet Ihr?
(trembling.)
Well then? What can I to you
Wo-für? Was kann ich Euch denn
trem.
pp
p
of-fer, Since by to-mor-row you
ge-ben, da Ihr doch mor-gen schon
(Pantomime of beheading.)
ANGELO. (with fire.)
My life for yours I
Ich ret-te Eu-er
f
proffer, If for reward you'll let me with your daugh-ter wed,
Le-ben: so ge-bet dann zum Lohn mir Eu-er Toch-ter Hand
CASTRUCCI. (perplexed.)
Why, you have lost your head!
Wie? seid Ihr bei Ver-stand?
What? you're as good as dead. Such
Wie? seid Ihr bei Verstand? Um
ANGELO.
mf

Allegro appassionato.
(passionately.)
prize is worth the win - ning, And death it - self I'll court, E'en
sol - chen Preis will tra - - gen ich je - des Miss - ge - schick. Und
Allegro appassionato. ♩ 160.
though at its be - gin - - ning, My bliss should be cut short,
sühlt auch kaum nach Ta - - gen mein kur - zes E - - he glück!
(fervidly.)
If I own her af - fec - - tion. Such sweet de-light 'twill be, I'll
Wenn Ri - ta mein ich nen - - ne, sei's nach so kur - - ze Zeit, dann
bear the rec - ol - lec - - tion, Thro' all e - ter - ni - ty, I'll
folgt mir Him - mels Won - - ne in Al - - - le E - wig - keit', dann
string.
cresc. e string.
bear the rec - ol - lec - - tion thro' all e - ter - ni - ty.
folgt mir Himmels - won - - ne in Al - - - le E - - wig - keit!

CASTRUCCI.
Young man you have gone wild, You can-not wed my child,
Das nenn' ich Schwärmerei! Das geht nicht jun-ger Mann!
ANG.
You will not? ve-ry well, Your heart is stern, but I can move it, The se-cret I will tell,
p poco a poco
f
con forza.
CASTRUCCI.
I rath-er think you'll have to prove it,
Das wer-det Ihr be-wei-sen müs-sen,
Yes cer-tain-ly you'll have to prove it.
das wer-det Ihr be-wei-sen müs-sen!
ANGELO. (showing a paper.)
By chance I have a pa-per here, Which seems to me a proof most clear; A
Der Zu-fall mach-te dies Pa-pier, als den Beweis zu ei-gen mir! Ein

Allegretto moderato. ♩=96.

(playfully.)

A pa-tent of no-bil-i-ty, To you from Duke of Med-i-ci, It real-ly seems to

A-delsbrief des Her-zogs seht, in welchem Eu-er Na-me steht, als des Ver-ra-thes

mf

me, You both must friend-ly be!

Preis; ein gül-ti-ger Be-weis!

CASTRUCCI. (anxious.)

Oh dear, what is it that I see, The

Er hat des Her-zogs A-delsbrief, o

p

thing looks awkward now for me!

je, jetzt geht die Sache schief!

ANGELO.

It really seems to me, That this the price of something great must

Er hat ihn Euch als Preis; ein gül-ti-ger und deut-li-cher Be-

mf

p

be!

weis!

p *p*

CASTRUCCI. (hesitating.)

But then my daughter?

Und mei-ne Toch-ter,

p

What says she?

was sagt die?

ANGELO.

I love her well, and she loves me. I

Sie liebt nur mich, ja mich al-lein! Ich

8

f *p*

swear that, if you don't a - gree, That by this time to - morrow,
schwör's: Wird sie nicht heut' noch mein, so neh - met Ihr schon morgen
In my place you'll be!
mei - ne Stel - le ein!
fz
p
m.g.
rall.
trem.
(teasing.)
pp
Shall
Soll
Assai moderato.
I to Fra Bom - bar - da go?
ich zu Fra Bom - bar - da gehn?
ritard. più a più.
Shall I this charming
Ein A - delsbrief des
pp
allargando.
let - ter show?
Her - zogs seht!
assai rit.
CASTRUCCI. (violently.)
ff
No!
Nein!
m.g.
ff
ffz
(faltering.)
Andante.
Since my daugh - ter loves you, be it so,
Da - mein Kind Euch liebt, so mag's gescheh'n;
(humorously.)
ANGELO.
I'm somewhat
Ihr wisst ja,
Andante.
p
f string.

112
Larghetto.
CASTRUCCI.
lim-i-ted in time dear fa-ther.
You
mei-ne Zeit ist sehr gemes-sen!
Larghetto.
p
p rit.
pp
(mopping his forehead.)
(whining.)
shall not be an hour a-part.
Your faithful love has touched my heart,
(aside.)
And Spara-ca-ni must have patience a lit-tle.
'Till death the pair shall
Und Spara-ca-ni muss in des-sen auch war-ten,
Allegro appassionato.
(fervidly.)
Yes death it-self I'm dar-ing,
For such a love-ly
part,
I care not what they will be say-ing,
At least in this I'll keep my head yes keep my
Allegro appassionato.
mf
pp
bride,
Tho' fate at once be tear-ing,
Her hus-band from her
head;
Not long with wedlock they'll be play-ing, for by to-morrow, by to-morrow he'll be

113
A
C
side!
glück!
If I own her af - fec - - - tion,
Wenn Ri - ta mein ich nen - - ne
dead, yes he'll be dead.
kann, nicht hel - fen kann.
His time is short, so I must haste to do the ma - ting.
Ach, sei - ne Zeit, ach sei - ne Zeit ist sehr ge - mes - sen;
p
Such sweet de - light 'twill be,
sei'n noch so kur - ze Zeit,
string.
I'll hear the re - col -
dann folgt mir Him - mels -
With - in an hour I'll wed the twain,
in näch - sten Stun - de sei's voll - führt,
And Spar - a - ca - ni must be
und Spa - ra - ca - ni muss in -
string.
- lec - - - - tion Thro' all e - ter - ni - ty,
won - - - - ne in al - - le E - wig - keit,
I'll
dann
kept a - wait - ing Till the wid - ow weds. Till she weds a - gain. Ah, yes!
dess' noch war - ten, bis sie Witt - we wird, bis sie Witt - we wird, ja, ja!
cresc. e string.
hear the re - col - lec - - tion Through all e - ter - ni -
folgt mir Him - mels won - - ne, in al - - le E - wig -
f
And Spara - ca - ni must be kept await - ing, must be kept awaiting, waiting Till she weds a -
Und Spara - ca - ni muss in dess' noch war - ten muss in - des' noch war - ten, warten, bis sie Witt - we
cresc. e string.
f

Più presto.
A
ff
-ty! The bliss of own-ing her af-fec-tion, Is re-ward e-nough for
keit! Nur sie, nur sie ist mei-ne Son-ne, ja bei ihr ist See-lig
C
ff
-gain, And Spa-ra-ca-ni must be kept a-wait-ing 'Till she weds a-
wird! Und Spa-ra-ca-ni muss in-dess' noch war-ten, bis sie Witt-we
ff
A
me, The bliss of own-ing her af-fec-tion, Is re-ward e-nough for
keit! Nur sie, nur sie ist mei-ne Son-ne, ja bei ihr ist See-lig-
C
-gain, And Spa-ra-ca-ni must be kept a-wait-ing 'Till she weds a-
wird und Spa-ra-ca-ni muss in-dess' noch war-ten bis sie Witt-we
A
me, e-nough for me!
keit, ja See-lig-keit!
C
-gain, Yes, weds a-gain!
wird, ja Witt-we wird!
con forza.
fz
ff

№ 10. Waltz Song

dim.
p
creep. — Thou must be to grief a stran - ger, I would ne'er cause thee to
stehn; — nur dein Lä-cheln will ich küs - sen, dei-ne Thrä - nen nim-mer
dim.
p
weep! — Hope can give strength, we may triumph at length. All troubles leav - ing,
sehn! — Hoff-nung giebt Muth, das das En-de noch gut, lässt kühn mich wa - gen,
mf
Gone is my griev - ing, For-tune can sometimes turn frown in-to smile. I will trust on yet a-
niemals ver - za - gen! Lacht doch dem Künstler For - tu - na so gern, drum will ich trau'n meinem
tr
- while! Ah!
Stern! Ja!
tr
pp
dolce.
Yes for thee a - lone I'm liv - ing, All my be - ing longs for thee! —
Mei - ne Lie - be ist mein Le - ben, ihr ge - hört mein gan - zes Sein —
p dolce.

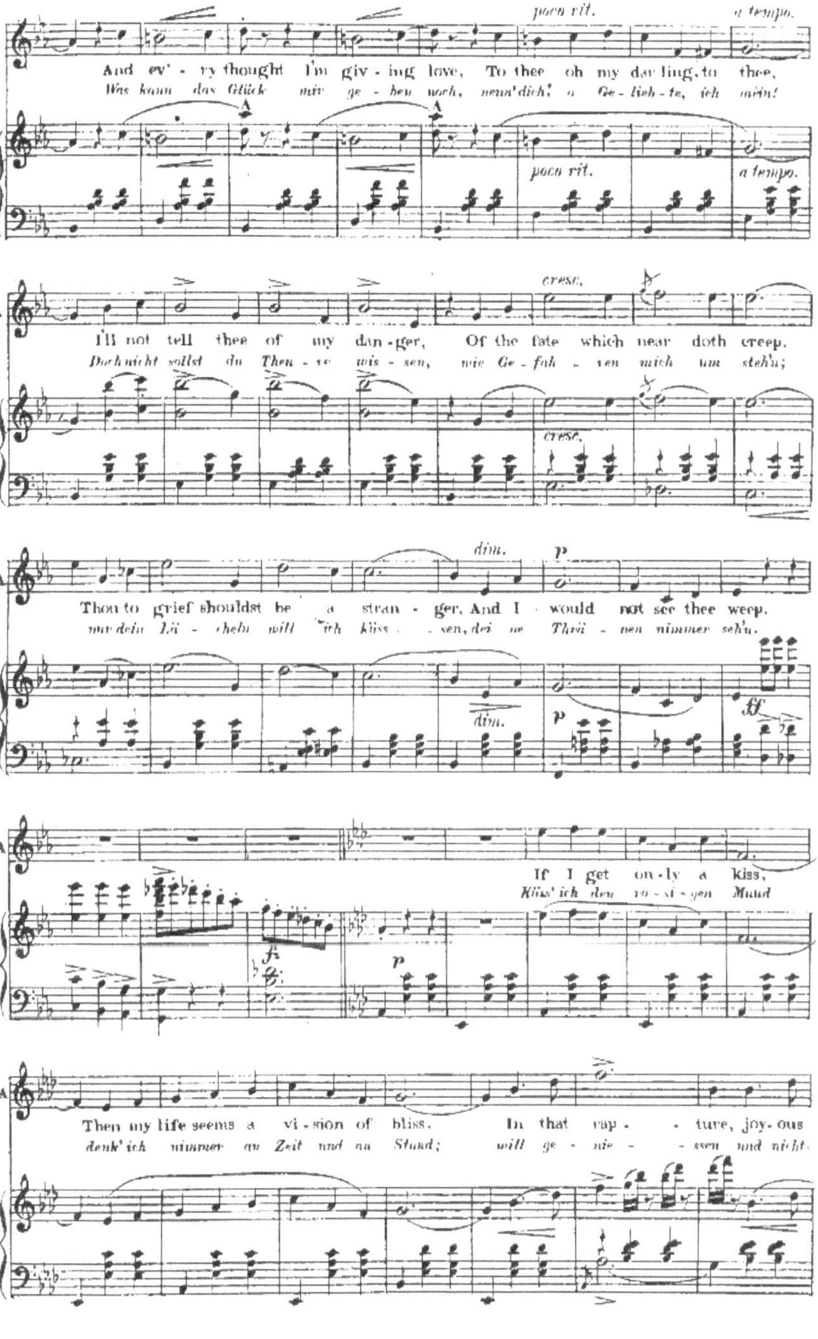
poco rit.
a tempo.
And ev'-ry thought I'm giv-ing love, To thee oh my dar-ling, to thee,
Was kann das Glück mir ge-ben noch, nenn' dich, o Ge-lieb-te, ich mein!
poco rit.
a tempo.
cresc.
I'll not tell thee of my dan-ger, Of the fate which near doth creep.
Doch nicht sollst du Treu-e wis-sen, wie Ge-fah-ren mich um steh'n;
cresc.
dim.
p
Thou to grief shouldst be a stran-ger, And I would not see thee weep.
nur dein Lä-cheln will ich küss-sen, dei-ne Thrä-nen nimmer seh'n.
dim.
p
ff
fz
p
If I get on-ly a kiss,
Küss' ich den ro-si-gen Mund
Then my life seems a vi-sion of bliss. In that rap-ture, joy-ous
denk' ich nimmer an Zeit und an Stund; will ge-nie-ssen und nicht

A
-heart - - ed, I'll not think how soon we must be part - - ed, In that bright
wis - - sen, ob wir mor - gen schon trennen uns müs - - sen! Ist doch der
f
rit.
ro - se - ate ray, — I'll en - joy thy sweet love while I may, — For in
Au - genblick mein, — wo mir strahlend im ro - si - gen Schein, — lacht die
rall. e dim.
f a tempo.
that heavenly smile and kiss Is a bliss, Driv - ing all care far a - way,
himm - lis - che See - lig - keit Tren - nungsleid, wirf kei - ne Schatten da - rein!
pp
p dolce.
Yes for thee a - lone I'm liv - ing, All my be - ing longs for thee, —
Meine Lie - be ist mein Le - ben, ihr ge - hört mein gan - zen Sein. —
poco rit.
a tempo.
— And ev' - ry thought I'm giv - ing love, To thee, oh my darling, to thee! —
— Was kann das Glück mir ge - ben noch nenn' dich, o Ge - lieb - te, ich mein. —

cresc.
I'll not tell thee of my dan-ger. Of the fate which near doth creep;
Doch nicht sollst du Theu-re wis-sen, wie Ge-fah-ren mich um steh'n;
rit.
Thou to grief shouldst be a stran-ger. And I would not see thee weep.
nur dein Lä-cheln will ich küs-sen, dei-ne Thrä-nen nim-mer seh'n!
Poco mosso.
If we can plight our vows so ten-der, I will not count the fear-ful
Darf um Al-ta-re ich dich füh-ren, strahlt in dem Ker-ker gold'-nes
cresc.
Quasi presto.
cost. And if I then must life sur-rend-er, I — shall not deem it lost. —
Licht. Muss ich das Le-ben auch ver-lie-ren, ver-lo-ren war es nicht! —
colla voce.

SINKING BEHIND THE BILLOW.

Words by Frank N. Scott. *MANDOLINA SERENADE.* Arr. by Wm. Gooch.

Allegretto grazioso.

f *sempre stacc.* *p leggierissimo.*

1. Sinking behind the billow See the sun seeks his pillow Bright dewdrops shine in radiance divine On flow'ret and droop-ing willow Now while the light is fading Under the leaf-y shading O-ver the mead-ow silent in shad-ow Come we in ser-e-nading La la la la la la la la. La la la la la la la la. Under the light that is shin-ing a-far Sing we now to the tink-ling light gui-tar Bright be thy way for-

2. Daylight is soft-ly dy-ing Ev'ning breez-es sighing Twilight is fall-ing night birds are call-ing As they are homeward flying So while the hours are winging Come we with mirthful singing List to our num-bers lulling thy slum-bers Life and its cares de-fy-ing La la la la la la la la. La la la la la la la la. Under the light &c

f *p* *f* *p* *f* *p*

ev_er Sorrow distress thee never Happy and free thy life ev_er be May
hap-pi_ness cheer thee ev_er Fortune and friends at_tending Pleasure with plen_ty
blending Light_ing thy way with ef_ful_gent ray 'Till life and love are o'er.
After 2d.Verse go to 2d.Chorus.
CHORUS FOR 1st.VERSE.
Sop.
Alto.
Love and hope gladden thy way With golden ray Be each joy free from al-
Ten.
Bass.
Love, hope, Love and hope,
loy Hope and joy! Over thy way in gold_en splendor
and joy,

C
No use re-sist-ing, It must be, It must be,
Du hilft kein Sträuben, er wird dein, er wird dein!
R
Re-sistance ne'er shall come from me, shall come from me.
Mich sträuben? Ha, fällt mir nicht ein fällt mir nicht ein
ANGELO.
Be-lov-ed thou'lt be mine yet to-
Ja, heu-te noch wirst du Theu-re
R
A
CASTRUCCI.
ANGELO.
day! It must be so, do as I say, My dearest thou my wife shalt be!
mein! Ich will es so, so soll es sein! Ge-lieb-te, ja, er willigt ein!
I
Kaum
ing.
p
ff
R
scarce can dream it, Wed with thee, I scarce could dream it, Scarce could dream it, wed with
kaum ich's glau-ben, er wird mein, kaum kaum ich's glauben, kaum ich's glau-ben, er wird
A
Yes darling he's con-sent-ed, And now mine thou'lt
Ge-lieb-te, ja, er wil-ligt ein, er wil-ligt
C
I wish it so and that's e-nough, So it must
Ich will es so, ich will es so, so soll es
f

R
thee, Wed with thee, Wed with thee, Wed with thee, Wed with thee!
mein! Er wird mein, er wird mein, er wird mein, er wird mein!
A
be, Mine thou'lt be, Mine thou'lt be, Mine thou'lt be, Mine thou'lt be!
ein! Wil ligt ein, wil ligt ein, wil ligt ein, wil ligt ein!
C
be, It must be, It must be, It must be, It must be!
sein! Soll es sein, soll es sein, soll es sein, soll es sein!
CASTRUCCI.
Allegretto.
Yes for you he wild was pleading,
Deine Hand von mir er-bat er!
ff
p
C
I his arguments was heeding, And I promised you should wed. It must be so, as I
said.
RITA.
Re-sistance you shall not see. To obey you, To o-bey you, Will my greatest pleasure be! Ah!
Ei, ich sag' gewiss nicht nein; deinen Willen zu-er-füllen, soll mir ein Vergnü-gen sein! Ja,
rit.
a piacere.
ANGELO.
Ah!
Ja,
f
p
colla parte.

123
Allegretto scherzando.
What a bliss is on me beam-ing, What a hap-pi-ness di-vine.
was ich kaum zu träu-men wag-te wird nun plötz-lich Wirk-lich-keit!
What a bliss is on me beam-ing, What a hap-pi-ness di-vine,
was ich kaum zu träu-men wag-te wird nun plötz-lich Wirk-lich-keit!
Allegretto scherzando. ♩=60.
That bright vi-sion of my dream-ing, Comes to pass and he is mine!
Er ist mein, die Heiss-ge-lieb-te, wel-che Him-mels-see-lig-keit!
That bright vi-sion of my dream-ing, Comes to pass and she is mine!
Sie ist mein, die Heiss-ge-lieb-te, wel-che Him-mels-see-lig-keit!
mf con amore.
Ah! what thought di-vine, I am whol-ly thine,
Al-les, was ich bin geb' ich ihm da-hin!
(aside.)
CASTRUCCI. On ma-tur-er re-flection, I don't like this af-
Auf wie lan-ge, wie lan-ge, mir wird ban-ge, wird
I shall bles-sed be, In thy love for me
da, er giebt da-für sei-ne Lie-be mir!
fection, I don't like this af-fec-tion. This af-fection
bange! Auf wie lange, wie lan-ge, mir wird bange!

appassionato.
Now our souls in joy are wing-ing, heavenward wing-ing. And our
Freu de leiht, ja Freu-de leiht der See - le Schwin-gen; ju - beln
ANGELO.
Now our souls in joy are wing-ing, heavenward wing-ing. And our
Freu - de leiht, ja Freu-de leiht der See - le Schwin-gen; ju - beln
L'istesso Tempo.
p
hearts are gai - ly sing-ing, Bright and gay the tones are ringing.
möcht ich, jauch-zen, sin - gen, weit, ja weit hinaussolls klingen!
cresc.
hearts are gai - ly sing-ing, Bright and gay the tones are ringing.
möcht ich, jauch-zen, sin - gen, weit, ja weit hinaussolls klingen!
cresc.
CASTRUCCI.
No, No, No! Oh, No, More slowly go; No, No, No! Oh, No, Don't shout it so!
Nein,nein,nein, o nein, das darf nicht sein; nein,nein,nein, o nein, das darf nicht sein!
pp
L'istesso Tempo.
(very softly.)
In a whis - per at the al - tar, You must an - swer soft - ly, "Yes!"
Nur ganz leis', so ist mein Wil - le, sprecht Ihr am Al - tar das "Ja!"
tr
pp

125
(very softly.)
R
Soft and low our ac - cents fal - ter, When we speak the bliss-ful
Nur ganz leis', so ist sein Wil - le, sa - gen am Al - tar das
A
Soft and low our ac - cents fal - ter, When we speak the bliss-ful
Nur ganz leis', so ist sein Wil - le, sa - gen am Al - tar das
C
When you speak the bliss-ful
Sprecht Ihr am Al - tar das
tr
Andante sostenuto.
Yes!
„Ja"
Ev'ry grief must now depart, Only joy our lot can bless.
Weit verweht ist je-der Schmerz! jedes Bangen floh dahin!
Andante sostenuto. ♩ 96.
pp
Ev-ry pain must now de - part.
Weit verweht ist je - der Schmerz
p
Perfect peace is in my heart; This at last is hap-pi - ness!
Fühl-le, wie mir pocht das Herz, fühle, wie ich selig bin!
Such stu-pid ass I nev-er did see!
Hat je man sol-chen Thoren gesehn?

126
126.
R
A
C
on-ly joy our lot can bless!
Je-des Ban-gen floh da-hin!
Per-fect peace is in my heart, — This at last is
Füh-le, wie mir pocht das Herz, — füh-le, wie ich
To-mor-row he be-head-ed will be,
Schon mor-gen um ihn geschehn;
hap-pi-ness, This at last is hap-pi-ness!
see-lig bin, füh-le, wie ich see-lig bin!
And yet he sings a-way! He's lost his head to-day, He's
Und heu-te singt er froh, als ging es im-mer so, als
On-ly joy our
Je-des Ban-gen
lives shall bless!
floh da hin!
con forza.
Thee at last
Du wirst mein,
lost his head to-day!
ging es im-mer so!
ff
m.g.
rall.
pp

127. Moderato.
RITA. (to Castrucci.)
127
bless - ing!
wähn - te!
legato.
But this wed - ding? 'Tis not
Die - se Hei - rath
CASTRUCCI.
play? There's no joke in such a way. Marriage is no cause for
Scherz? In der Eh' giebt's keinen Scherz, ernsthaft ist's ganz fürchter -
jest
lich
(aside.)
Of all men I know that best!
Wer weiss be - ser das, als ich?
colla parte.
Allegro scherzando. ♩=60.
What new bliss is on me beam - ing, What a hap - pi - ness di - vine!
Was ich kaum zu träu - men wag - te wird nun plötz - lich Wirk - lich - keit!
What new bliss is on me beam - ing, What a hap - pi - ness di - vine!
Was ich kaum zu träu - men wag - te wird nun plötz - lich Wirk - lich - keit!
That bright vis - ion of my dream - ing, Comes to pass and she is mine!
Er ist mein, der Heiss - ge - lieb - te, wel - che Him - mels - see - lig - keit!
That bright vis - ion of my dream - ing, Comes to pass and she is mine!
Sie ist mein, die Heiss - ge - lieb - te, wel - che Him - mels - see - lig - keit!

mf con amore.
Ah, what thought di - vine! I am whol - ly
Al - les, was ich bin geb' ich ihm da -
(aside)
CASTRUCCI. On ma - tur - er re - flec - tion,
Auf wie lan - ge, wie lan - ge,
mf
thine! I shall bless - ed be,
hin! Ja, er giebt da - für
I don't like this af - fec - tion! I don't like this af -
mir wird ban - ge, wird ban - ge! Auf wie lan - ge wie
f
fz
In thy love for me!
sei - ne Lie - be mir!
appassionato.
Now our souls in
Freu - de leiht, ja
ANGELO.
- fec - tion, This af - fec - tion!
ban - ge, mir wird ban - ge!
Now our souls in
Freu - de leiht, ja
L'istesso Tempo.
p
joy are wing - ing, heav'n - ward wing - ing, And our hearts are
Freu - de leiht der See - le Schwin - gen; ju - beln möcht' ich,
joy are wing - ing, heav'n - ward wing - ing, And our hearts are
Freu - de leiht der See - le Schwin - gen; ju - beln möcht' ich,

129.
129
R
gai - ly sing - ing, Loud and clear - the tones are ring-ing,
jauch - zen sin - gen, weit, ja weit hin-aus soll's klin - gen!
A
gai - ly sing - ing, Loud and clear the tones are ring-ing,
jauch - zen sin - gen, weit, ja weit hin-aus soll's klin - gen!
CASTRUCCI
No, No, No, oh, no! More soft-ly go, No, no, no, oh, no!
Nein, nein, nein, o nein, das darf nicht sein; nein, nein, nein, o nein,
pp
C
Don't shout it so,
das darf nicht sein!
pp
Don't shout it so,
Das darf nicht sein!
pp morendo.
R
ppp
At the al - tar whis - per "yes!"
Spre - chen am Al - tar das "Ja!"
A
ppp
At the al - tar whis - per "yes!"
Spre - chen am Al - tar das "Ja!"
C
ppp
Don't shout it so!
das darf nicht sein!
m.g.
ppp

№12. FINALE II.

131.
131
Picc.
Viol.
6143 + 191

SOPRANI.
ff
Let them be welcome! Give the strangers cordial greet - ing! Still grander
Heisst sie will-kommen, grü-sset laut die Frem-den Gä - ste! Pracht, Glanz und
TENORI.
FORTEBRACCIO col Ten I.
ff
Let them be welcome! Give the strangers cordial greet - ing! Still grander
Heisst sie will-kommen, grü-sset laut die Frem-den Gä - ste! Pracht, Glanz und
BASS.
ff
CHOR.
is our feast be-cause of this strange meet - ing. Hail Mo-roc-co! Hail Mo-
Schimmer lei - hen heu - te sie dem Fe - ste! Hoch Ma - roc - co! Hoch Ma-
is our feast be-cause of this strange meet - ing. Hail Mo-roc-co! Hail Mo-
Schimmer lei - hen heu - te sie dem Fe - ste! Hoch Ma - roc - co! Hoch Ma-
-roc-co! Hail, hail, hail!
roc- co! Hoch, hoch, hoch!
-roc-co! Hail, hail, hail!
roc- co! Hoch, hoch, hoch!

133. Moderato.
FRA BOMBARDA.
133
A good i - dea! He can keep mum! A dip - lomat that's
Höchst praktisch scheint mir in der That, ein stum - mer Di - plo -
dolce.
Fr. B.
dumb!
Most statesmen ought to wear a gag, Their tongues too freely wag.
mat!
Der, wenn man noch so pfiffig fragt, nie ei - ne Dummheit sagt! (dumb.)
AMBASSADOR.
A
p
Fr. B.
The art of pan - tomime he'll teach.
Im stummen Spiel scheint er ge - übt.
A
Fr. B.
A ve - ry non-committal speech!
Das kan man nehmen wie's beliebt!
mf
fz

134
Allegretto.
FORTERRACCIO.
He begs your ex-cel-lence to view. The female slaves he's
Es bit-tet sei-ne Ex-cellenz die Skla-vin-nen sich
p
FRA BOMBARDA.
brought for you: A present which he hopes you'll take.
an-zuschaun, die als Geschenk er mit gebracht!
I'm much obliged.
Sehr ob-ligirt!
GESANDTER. Recit.
Well for his sake I'll take the present and the slaves he's brought.
Ich muss gestehn, dass sol-che Ga-ben ich be-son-ders schätz'!
m m m
m m m
tr
f
Recit.
Fag.
FORTERRACCIO.
m m m m m m m m m!—
m m m m m m m m!—
They were the best in Fez that could be
Das schön-ste was zu ha-ben war in
pp
rit.
Moderato con moto. ♩=88.
SLAVES.
bought.
Fez!
To men we always must belong, We
Wir sind der Männer Ei-genthum, ihr
f
ff m.d.
p

1634+15

135.
135
are at their command;
Wil - le ist Ge - setz;
We hope you do not think it wrong, Tis custom in our
so sind's gewohnt von Jugend auf, die Mädchen all' aus
kei - nen Mann uns ab
men with trick and art,
land!
Fez!
To catch the men with fairy art, We do not under-
Wir fan-gen kei-nen Mann uns ab im gold'-nen Liebes-
uns damit nicht Müh'
bo - dy soul and heart,
stand!
netz!
They buy us body, soul and heart. Tis cus - tom in our
Wir ge-hen uns damit nicht Müh', das thut man nicht in
land.
Fez!
We do not fool our time a-way In balls or parties
Wir pu - tzen uns den gan zen Tag, das ist die einz'ge
grand;
Hetz;
We dress and eat, the livelong day, Tis custom in our land!
Fez!

FR.BOMB.
FORTEBR.
Piu mosso.
We like the style, we like the style, The cus-toms of their land! We like the style, we
So le-ben sie, so le-ben sie, so le - ben sie in Fez! So le-ben sie, so
like the style, The cus-toms of their land! Their land, their land!
le-ben sie, so le - ben sie in Fez! In Fez! In Fez!
CHOR.
Fr.B
F
6
S

137
Allegro moderato.
FRA BOMBARDA.
137
We need the wom-en ve - ry bad-ly, We take the
Es könnt uns solch Geschenk ge-le-gen, wir brauchen
pp
Tempo di
Fr. B
present them, of course, For recent laws have been en-act-ed, Which make it ea-sy for di - vorce.
Frau-en mehr als je! Danach den neu en Staatsge-setzen ward auf-ge-löst so manche Eh'!
Mazurka. ♩=132.
AMBASS.
m m m m m m m m m m
FRA BOMBARDA.
One, Fortebraccio I pres-ent you,
Du, Forte-braccio, hast du Ei - ne!
Fr. B
Count, this young la-dy will content you, Here Moro you take number
Graf A - sin - el - li kriegt die Klei - ne; Für Moro passet diese
rit.
a tempo.
Fr. B
three, The others please reserve for me.
hier; Die Drei da re - ser - vir' ich mir!
rit.
a tempo.

138
Fr. B
A pretty present as I live,
Now something I will al-so do,
138
This present in re-turn I'll give,
nehmt die ge-schied'nen Wei-ber hin.
Take our divorced wives back with you,
die uns hier ü-ber-zäh-lig sind.
Allegro molto.
(PERPETUA
No!
Nein!
AMB. (excitedly.)
(more and more agitated.)
and divorced women.)
P. & WOM.
To Mo-roc-co we won't go!
Nach Ma-roc-co geh'n wir nie!
FR., BOMB. & FORTEBRACCIO.
What is it now? Why grunts he so?
Was hat er nur, verschmäht er sie?
(angrily.)
A

139.
139
G
m m m m m m m m m m m m m m m m m m m m
dim.
Allegretto.
FRA BOMBARDA.
m'
pp
His mean-ing, His meaning I can on-ly
Noch Dun-kel, noch Dun-kel scheint mir was er
Fr. B
guess. But one things ve-ry clear. It is not
spricht; nur Eins, nur Eins ist klar er will sie
Allegro.
ff
"yes," But one thing's clear, he won't say "yes," He won't say "yes," He don't say "yes,"
nicht, nur Eins ist klar, er will sie nicht; er will sie nicht, er will sie nicht!
FORTEBR.
But one thing's clear, he won't say "yes," He won't say "yes," He don't say "yes,"
Nur Eins ist klar, er will sie nicht; er will sie nicht, er will sie nicht!
(PERPETUA and several women.)
But one thing's clear, he won't say "yes," He won't say "yes," He don't say "yes,"
Er will uns nicht er will uns nicht; er will uns nicht, er will uns nicht!
CHORUS
But one thing's clear, he won't say "yes," He won't say "yes," He don't say "yes,"
Er will sie nicht er will sie nicht; er will sie nicht, er will sie nicht!
But one thing's clear, he won't say "yes," He won't say "yes," He don't say "yes,"
Er will sie nicht er will sie nicht; er will sie nicht, er will sie nicht!

140
Fr. B
I thought the thing I'd try, I do not won-der you re-fuse;
Ich bit-te zu ver-zeih'n, dass soll kein' ve-sus hel-li sein;
p
f
Fr. B
I don't blame you a bit, I hope the in-sult you'll ex-
ich bit-te zu ver-zeih'n, das soll kein re-sus hel-li
p
Fr. B
cuse, And do not let your wrath get hot.
sein, be-leid'-gen wollt' ich durch-aus nicht!
F
ff
He wants them not, He wants them not.
Er will sie nicht er will sie nicht!
P & W
ff
He wants us not, He wants us not.
Er will uns nicht, er will uns nicht!
ff
He wants them not, He wants them not.
Er will sie nicht, er will sie nicht!
ff
He wants them not, He wants them not.
Er will sie nicht, er will sie nicht!
ff
fz
fz
Adagio.
(Organ behind the scenes.)
p
Allegro maestoso. 𝅗𝅥=108
pesante.
ff

Fr. B
F
A
P & W
CHOR
m m m m m m m m
Hail the new-ly wed-ded pair! Let us bring them greetings
Heil, dem neu-ver-mähl-ten Paar! brin - get ih-nen Wünsche
fair! The cer-e-mony now is done, The blushing pair are one!
dar! Sie kehren vom Al-tar zu-rück, es blüh' ihr jun-ges Glück!
ff
p

142
Andante cantabile.
142
Fr. B
pp (aside.)
CASTRUCCI.
How fair she is!
Wie ist sie schön!
You're wedded
Sie sind ver-
p
C
now,
mählt!
Re-turn your thanks.
Bedankt Euch nun!
tr
RITA.
To you we kneel.
Wir dan - ken sehr!
ANGELO.
To you we kneel.
Wir dan - ken sehr!
FRA BOMB.
(aside)
f
A bit-ter vengeance do I
Das hat mir grade noch ge-
AMBASSADOR.
(GESANDTER.)
m m m m m m m m m m m!
Allegro maestoso.
Allegro maestoso.
pesante.
ff
Fr. B
vow!
fehlt;
I scarce can hide the rage I feel!
kaum ber - ge mei-nen Zorn ich mehr!

143.
143
AMBASS.
m mmmmmm
mmmmmmm
PERPETUA and WOMEN.
Hail, the newly wedded pair, Let us bring them greetings fair, The
Heil, dem neuvermählten Paar! Brin - get ihn - en Wünsche dar! Sie
Hail, the newly wedded pair, Let us bring them greetings fair, The
Heil, dem neuvermählten Paar! Brin - get ihn - en Wünsche dar! Sie
Hail, the newly wedded pair, Let us bring them greetings fair, The
Heil, dem neuvermählten Paar! Brin - get ihn - en Wünsche dar! Sie
CHOR.
ff
cer-e-mony now is done, The blushing twain are one, The twain are one.
kehren vom Altar zürück, es blüh' ihr jun - ges Glück! Ihr jun - ges Glück!
cer-e-mony now is done, The blushing twain are one, The twain are one.
kehren vom Altar zürück, es blüh' ihr jun - ges Glück! Ihr jun - ges Glück!
cer-e-mony now is done, The blushing twain are one, The twain are one.
kehren vom Altar zürück, es blüh' ihr jun - ges Glück! Ihr jun - ges Glück!
f
ff
p

Allegro non troppo.

145.
Fr. B
sor - ry for dis - turb - ing so Your hap - pi-ness, but you must go
stö - ren un - gern Eu - er Glück; doch folg - sam dem Ge - setz zu sein:
Fr. B
Back to your pri - son cell be - low.
Kehrt in den Ker - ker jetzt zu - rück!
ff
RITA.
I'll go with him!
Ich geh' mit ihm!
R
I'll go with him!
Ich geh' mit ihm!
Fr. B
ff
I must say no! No, no! In
Das geht nicht, nein! Nein, nein! Man
Fr. B
pri - son cell A - lone he'll dwell.
sperr ihn ein, und zwar al - lein!

RITA.
Let mer-cy in your bosom dwell!
O wol-let Gna-de ihm ver-leih'n,
Let mer-cy in your bosom
o wol-let Gna-de ihm ver-
Fr. B
No, take him to his pri-son cell!
Das kaŭ nicht sein, hi-nein, hi-nein!
FORTERRACCIO.
F
CASTRUCCI.
P & W
dwell!
leih'n!
R
C
ff
rit.
6173-101

Tempo di Valse. (♩. = 56)
SPARACANI
p
Well here we are
Da sind wir schon!
a tempo
poco rit.
pp
I've come a lit - tle late
Mir scheint, ich komm' zu spät!
AMBASSADOR
m m m m m m m
You must ex-cuse
Man harrt auf mich,
E'en if you had for me to wait
ach wie die Zeit so schnell ver - geht!
Now forward
Nur vorwärts,
Let us go
bit - te ich!
CASTR.
Where to? Let's tar-ry.
Wo - hin so schnelle?
SPARAC.
Where to?
Wo - hin?
S
A
m m m m m m m
To church, To marry, Come let us go a - head.
Als zur Ca-pel-le! Mit Ri-ta, mei - ner Braut!

148
148.
ANGELO.
Ri - ta's al - rea - dy wed.
Die ist be - reits ge - traut!
SPARAC.
Is wed? With who?
Ge - traut? Mit wem?
Fra BOMB.
With Angelo!
Mit Angelo
S.
With You?
Mit dem?
CASTRUCCIO.
Si - lent - ly this endure, Else we are gone up sure.
Macht kei - ne Ne - de - rei, sonst ist's mit uns vor - bei!
SPARAC.
But I?
Doch ich?
CASTR.
hush!
Schweigt!
SPAR
And she?
Doch sie?
CASTR.
Shut up!
So schweigt!
C
This night with An - ge - lo she'll sup, But in the morn, off goes his head.
und kei - ne Ü - ber - ra - schung zeigt; schon morgen ist's um ihn ge - schehn!
cresc. - poco a - poco
S
And then?
Und dann?
C
Per - haps you may wed!
Dann wol - len wir sehn!
f
Allegro.
fz

149.
149
RITA
He's puzzled quite See, oh see He don't know how this can
ANGELO.
Er ist per-plex! Seht nur seht, der Ver-stand ihm stil-le
FR. BOMB.
FORTEBR.
He's puzzled quite See, oh see He don't know how this can
CASTR.
Er ist per-plex! Seht nur seht, der Ver-stand ihm stil-le
A
m m m m m m m m m m m m m m m m m m
CHOR.
PERP. & WOMEN. He's puzzled quite See, oh see He don't know how this can
col Sopr. I. & II. Er ist per-plex! Seht nur seht, der Ver-stand ihm stil-le
R
be He's puzzled quite See, oh see He can't tell why this should be.
steht! Er ist per-plex! Seht nur, seht, der Ver-stand ihm stil-le steht!
A
Fr B F
be He's puzzled quite See, oh see He can't tell why this should be.
steht! Er ist per-plex! Seht nur, seht, der Ver-stand ihm stil-le steht!
C
A
m!
be He's puzzled quite See, oh see He can't tell why this should be.
steht! Er ist per-plex! Seht nur, seht, der Ver-stand ihm stil-le steht!
ff
pp
Tempo di Valse.
6173-191

R
Too late you've come my friend The wedding now is at an end Up-
Zu spät kommt Ihr hier an, schon ist die Hoch zeit ab ge than! Es
A
Fr
B
F
Ha ha ha!
Ha ha ha!
C
Ha ha ha!
Ha ha ha!
A
Ha ha ha!
Ha ha ha!
on your wed-ding day Your bride is sto-len swift a-way It real-ly
schnappt die Braut Euch keck ein And'rer vor der Na se weg! Das ist ein
pp

6173-191

151
poco a poco
is too bad No won-der that you're ve-ry sad Do not fret yourself
gross Mal-heur und wir be-dau-ern Al-le sehr; Doch macht Euch nicht viel
Ha ha ha!
Ha ha ha!
Ha ha ha!
Ha ha ha!
Ha ha ha!
Ha ha ha!
poco a poco
cresc.
so, For fretting won't mend it, you know. Too late you've come my friend
draus, die Sa-che ist nun einmal aus Zu spät komt Ihr hier an
Ha ha ha! Too late, too late you've come
Ha ha ha! Zu spät zu spät komt Ihr
Ha ha ha! mm mm mm mm m
Ha ha ha! Too late you've come my friend
Ha ha ha! Zu spät komt Ihr hier an
Ha ha ha! Too late, too late you've come
Ha ha ha! Zu spät zu spät komt Ihr
cresc.

152
152.
B
The wedding now is at an end Upon your wedding
schon ist die Hochzeit abgethan! Es schnappt die Braut Euch
A
Fr B F
my friend, The wedding now is at an end Upon, upon
hier an, schon ist die Hochzeit abgethan! Es schnappt es schnappt
C
A
m m m m m m m m m m! m m m m
The wedding now is at an end Upon, your wedding
schon ist die Hochzeit abgethan! Es schnappt die Braut Euch
my friend, The wedding now is at an end Upon, upon
hier an, schon ist die Hochzeit abgethan! Es schnappt es schnappt
B
day Your bride was boldly stole away Alas, It is too
keck ein And'rer vor der Nase weg! Das ist ein gross Mal-
A
Fr B F
your wedding day Your bride was stolen bold away Alas, Alas
die Braut Euch keck, ein And'rer vor der Nase weg! Das ist, das ist
C
A
m m m m m m m m m m m m m m m
day Your bride was boldly stole away Alas, It is too
keck ein And'rer vor der Nase weg! Das ist ein gross Mal-
your wedding day Your bride was stolen bold away Alas, Alas
die Braut Euch keck, ein And'rer vor der Nase weg! Das ist, das ist
6178-491

153
153
R
bad No won-der that you're ve - ry sad Do not fret yourself
heur und wir be - dau-ern al - le sehr, doch macht Euch nicht viel
A
Fr
B
F
It is too bad No wonder that you're ve-ry sad No use in
ein gross Malheur und wir be - dau-ern al - le sehr; doch macht Euch
C
A
m m m m m m m m m m m; m m m
bad No won-der that you're ve-ry sad Do not fret yourself
heur und wir be dau - ern al - le sehr, doch macht Euch nicht viel
It is too bad No wonder that you're ve-ry sad No use in
ein gross Malheur und wir be - dau-ern al - le sehr; doch macht Euch
R
so, For fret-ting won't mend, for fretting won't mend it, you know.
d'raus, die Sa-che ist aus, die Sa che ist nun ein-mal aus!
A
Fr
B
F
fretting so, Fretting won't mend it, No won't mend it, you know
nicht viel d'raus, die Sa-che ist nun aus, ist nun ein - mal aus!
C
A
m m m m m m m m m m m m m m!
so, For fret-ting won't mend, for fretting won't mend it, you know.
d'raus, die Sa - che ist aus, die Sa-che ist nun ein - mal aus!
fretting so, - Fretting won't mend it, No won't mend it, you know.
nicht viel d'raus, die Sa-che ist nun aus, ist nun ein - mal aus!
ff
P legato
6173 - 191

SPARAC.
Yes _ though they are wed; Still all our hope has not yet fled: For to-morrow he
Ja _ bei al - ler Pein bleibt der Trost nur al - lein: Dass es morgen schon
los-es his head. Now back to prison swift must he.
an-ders wird sein! doch in den Kerker nun auf's Neu'!
RITA.
Tear not a - part the newly wed - ded.
Ihr sollt mich nicht von ihm ver - drän - gen!
Now back to pris - on swift must he.
doch in den Ker - ker nun auf's Neu'!
Oh, give him mer - cy, let him free.
O, übt doch Gna - de lasst ihn frei!
CHOR.
Tear not a
Ihr sollt mich

155.
FRA BOMB.
155
R
part the newly wed-ded!
nicht von ihm ver-drän-gen!
I'd like to have them both be-headed! Still
Am Liebsten lies ich Bei-de hangen! Bei
C
Let him free!
Lasst ihn frei!
Let him free!
Lasst ihn frei!
p
f
SPARAC.
Fr B
I am pleased, mid all the strife, That this old block-head lost his wife. He's wedded
al-le-dem bin ich ver-gnügt, dass die-ser Dumm-kopf sie nicht kriegt. Er ist mit
Fl.
p
colla parte
RITA
ANGELO
Ha ha ha ha ha ha ha ha ha ha! Too
Ha ha ha ha ha ha ha ha ha ha! Zu
FRA BOMB.
FORTEBR.
Ha ha ha ha ha ha ha ha ha ha! Too
Ha ha ha ha ha ha ha ha ha ha! Zu
S
with my promised wife, Who heard the like in all his life!
mei-ner Braut vermählt, das hat noch zum Mal-heur ge-fehlt!
Too
Zu
CASTR.
Ha ha ha ha ha ha ha ha ha ha! Too
Ha ha ha ha ha ha ha ha ha ha! Zu
Ha ha ha ha ha ha ha ha ha ha! Too
Ha ha ha ha ha ha ha ha ha ha! Zu
CHOR.
ff
cresc. assai e string.

156.
R
A
late you've come my friend The wed-ding now is at an end Up-
spät kommt Ihr hier an, schon ist die Hoch-zeit ab-ge-than! Es
Fr
B
F
late you've come my friend The wed-ding now is at an end Up-
spät kommt Ihr hier an, schon ist die Hoch-zeit ab-ge-than! Es
S
late you've come my friend The wed-ding now is at an end Up-
spät kommt Ihr hier an, schon ist die Hoch-zeit ab-ge-than! Es
C
late you've come my friend The wed-ding now is at an end Up-
spät kommt Ihr hier an, schon ist die Hoch-zeit ab-ge-than! Es
ff
R
A
on your wed-ding day Your bride is sto-len swift a-way It
schnappt die Braut Euch keck, ein And'-rer vor der Na-se weg; es
Fr
B
F
on your wed-ding day Your bride is sto-len swift a-way It
schnappt die Braut Euch keck, ein And'-rer vor der Na-se weg; es
S
on your wed-ding day Your bride is sto-len swift a-way It
schnappt die Braut Euch keck, ein And'-rer vor der Na-se weg; es
C
on your wed-ding day Your bride is sto-len swift a-way It
schnappt die Braut Euch keck, ein And'-rer vor der Na-se weg; es

157.
157
sempre - piu - - cresc.
R
A
really is too bad — No wonder that you're — very sad —
ist ein gross Malheur — und wir bedauern — Alle sehr; —
Fr
B
F
really is too bad — No wonder that you're — very sad —
ist ein gross Malheur — und wir bedaueru — Alle sehr; —
S
really is too bad — No wonder that I'm — very sad —
ist ein gross Malheur — und zu bedauern — Alle sehr; —
C
really is too bad — No wonder that you're very sad —
ist ein gross Malheur — und wir bedauern — Alle sehr; —
really is too bad — No wonder that you're — very sad —
ist ein gross Malheur — und wir bedauern — Alle sehr; —
cresc.
sempre piu cresc.
R
A
— Do not fret yourself then so — It cannot be help'd now you
— doch macht Euch nicht — viel daraus, — die Sache ist nun einmal
Fr
B
F
— Do not fret yourself then so — It cannot be help'd now you
doch macht Euch nicht — viel daraus, — die Sache ist nun einmal
S
— Do not fret yourself then so — It cannot be help'd now you
zu bedauern — bin ich sehr, — ich führe die Braut nach nach
C
— Do not fret yourself then so — It cannot be help'd now you
— doch macht Euch nicht — viel daraus, — die Sache ist nun einmal
— Do not fret yourself then so — It cannot be help'd now you
— doch macht Euch nicht — viel daraus, — dir Sache ist nun einmal
f
fz rit.
ff

158
158.
Presto.
R A
know. It is quite too bad. 'Twas
aus! Welch' ein gross Mal - heur Ar -
Fr B F
know. It is quite too bad. 'Twas
aus! Welch' ein gross Mal - heur Ar -
S
know. It is quite too bad. 'Twas
Haus! Welch' ein gross Mal - heur Ich
C
know. It is quite too bad. 'Twas
aus! Welch' ein gross Mal - heur Ar -
know. It is quite too bad. 'Twas
aus! Welch' ein gross Mal - heur Ar -
ff
Presto.
R A
mis - for - tune great That you came just too late That you
mer Bräu - ti - gam der zu spät lei - der kam, der zu
Fr B F
mis - for - tune great That you came just too late That you
mer Bräu - ti - gam der zu spät lei - der kam, der zu
S.
mis - for - tune great That I came too late too
führ' nicht nach Haus, ich führ' nicht die Braut nach,
C
mis - for - tune great That you came just too late That you
mer Bräu - ti - gam der zu spät lei - der kam, der zu
mis - for - tune great That you came just too late That you
mer Bräu - ti - gam der zu spät lei - der kam, der zu
8

R
A
came too late. Ha ha ha ha ha ha ha ha ha ha ha ha!
spät heut' kam! Ha ha ha ha ha ha ha ha ha ha ha ha!
Fr
B
F
came too late. Ha ha ha ha ha ha ha ha ha ha ha ha!
spät heut' kam! Ha ha ha ha ha ha ha ha ha ha ha ha!
S
late.
Haus!
C
came too late. Ha ha ha ha ha ha ha ha ha ha ha ha!
spät heut' kam! Ha ha ha ha ha ha ha ha ha ha ha ha!
came too late. Ha ha ha ha ha ha ha ha ha ha ha ha!
spät heut' kam! Ha ha ha ha ha ha ha ha ha ha ha ha!
ff
fz
fff
End of 2d Act.

III. ACT.

Nº 13. Introduction, Air and Duet.

Melodram.
L'istesso tempo.
trem.
Cadenza.
rit.
Andantino. ♩=88.
RITA.
He slumbers so soft, He smiles in his dream,
Er schlummert so süss, er lächelt im Traum,
No danger he dreads, quite calm doth he seem;
Es stört die Gefahr den Frieden ihm kaum;
My An-ge - lo.
mein An-ge - lo!
swaying.
And yet I
Und doch fühl'
Allegro molto moderato.

162
R
deep - - - ly am fear - - - - ing, I
heim - - - lich ich Grau - - - en: Ich
saw with keen an - - - ger blaz - - - - ing, The
sah des Ty - ran - - - nen Bli - - - cke mit
ty - rant at him gaz - - - - ing, The
Lä - cheln, doch voll Tü - - - cke auf
glance of wi - ly hate, I know it forebodes some dark
uns her - nie - der schau'n! Und muss die - sem Lächeln miss -
cresc.
fate.
trau'n!
Meno.
He grant - ed my pray'r with a
Wohl gab mei - nem Flehn er Ge -
f
rit.
fp

163.
165
smile; Re-leased him from his prison cell but to hide some dark
hor: Der Ker-kers düst-re Nacht um-fängt den Ge-leib-ten nicht
wile. The dungeon holds him not, Yet fear I some dark hidden
mehr, und ihm bald Freiheit lacht! Doch sind wir von fern noch be-
plot, And he my An-ge-lo!
wacht! Und er, mein An-ge-lo!
Andantino. ♩ = 48.
He slumbers so soft,
Er schlum̄ert so süss,
He smiles in his dream, No
er lächelt im Traum; Es
danger he dreads, But tranquil doth seem. My An-ge-lo!
stört die Ge-fahr den Frie-den ihm kaum; mein An-ge-lo!

164 Duett: FRA BOMBARDA. (aside.) 164.
At last I can meet her, What luck that she's here,
Da ist sie im Gar_ten, das trifft sich ja schön!
I'll ten_der_ly greet her, And gen_tle ap_pear;
Ich konnt's nicht er war_ten sie wie_der zu seh'n!
Al_though I have num_bered My ri_val's sweet hours,
Denn sind auch dem Frer_ter die Stun_de ge_zählt,
(agitated.)
My heart is en_cum_bered In jeal_ous_y's pow'rs.
von Ei_fer_sucht füh_le mein Herz, ich ge_quält!
Allegretto.
This must close to here
Nun wohl_an, frisch her.
pp Ped.
6173=191

165.
166
Fr
B
(sweetly)
Allegro.
goes.
aus!
Fair-est Ri - ta!
Hol - de Ri - ta!
RITA (in fright)
Who is here?
Was wollt Ihr?
Come not near!
Fort von hier!
FRA BOMB.
Ah ha, my dear Are these the thanks you give
Ei, ei, mein Schatz! Ist das der Dank da - für,
That I your An-ge-lo al - lowed to live And eased your heart of
dass ich durch Eu-er Fleh'n mich rühren liess, und An - ge - lo nicht
great distress, and fear.
in den Ker - ker stiess!
RITA
Shh, be still!
Pst! Nur still!
6172 - 194

Andantino.
R
He slumbers so soft, He smiles in his dream, He
Er schlummert so süss, er lä - chelt im Traum, er
FRA BOMB. (scornfully)
pp
He slumbers so soft, He
Er schlummert so süss, er
Andantino.
f
pp
smiles in his dream! My An-ge - lo!
lä - chelt im Traum! Mein An - ge - lo!
Fr B
smiles in his dream!
lä - chelt im Traum!
p
Your
Ich
Allegretto moderato scherzando.
ff
thanks on me should now descend
zähl' auf dei - ne Dankbarkeit!
Yes all my thanks to you shall be When you have set him
Ja, inn'-ger Dank sei Euch geweiht wenn Ihr ihm ganz die
wholly free
Freiheit schenkt!
(aside)
rit.
a tempo
(to Rita)
To - day of him I'll make an end.
Noch heu - te wird der Kerl ge - hängt!
You can - not be so
Doch darfst du nicht so
con espressione
colla parte
f
a tempo

167.
RITA (aside)
167
Fr B
hursh to me.
grau-sam sein.
Yes, I must friendly to him be.
Ich muss ja freundlich mit ihm sein;
pp rit.
a piacere
R
Love pretend-ing,
muss ihm schmeicheln,
Glances sending,
Lie-be her-cheln;
Strong and great is his
mäch-tig ist der Ty-
colla voce
pp
fs
might,
rann,
Yes, he could crush us quite.
der uns ver-der-ben kann!
rit.
FRA BOMB.
Allegro energico
Now her looks somewhat kinder grow,
Sie bli-cket mich ver-hei-ssend an,
To the charge now let us go,
nun wohl-an, fan-gen wir an!
Now at-tack her
Zur At-ta-que
strong and bold, She may not be very cold.
Ah how
Ach, wie
m.g.
pp
rall.
dol.

Andante grazioso. (♩ = 84)
R
Fr
B
sad was I When thou wert not nigh; For since yester-day From me thou'st
bang war mir, fern so lang von dir; sah seit gestern nicht, dein hol-des
think and do 'Tis with thee in view, Thou my joy or woe Canst bid to
Denk und thu, lässt mir kei-ne Ruh'. seit ich dir ge-weiht dies Herz voll
been a-way. All my thoughts will flee Day and night to thee, And I
An-ge-sicht! Weil ich Nacht und Tag dein nur Den-ken mag und vor
cease or flow. Nothing can en-trance Like your beam-ing glance, And it
Zärt-lich-keit! Bin in dei-nem Bann, blickt dein Aug' mich an, muss ich
pp
But more soft-ly, For my
A-ber lei-se A-ber
rit.
seem to die When thou'rt not by.
Lieb' ver-geh' in dei-ner Näh'!
would be bliss If I took a kiss.
auch zur Stund' küssen dei-nen Mund!
pp
Yes more soft-ly,
A-ber lei-se
Yes more soft-ly,
A-ber lei-se
colla parte
morendo pp

169.
sake That the hus-band you do not a-wake.
sacht, dass der Gat-te nicht vom Schlaf er-wacht.
for your sake, That the hus-band I do not a-wake.
a-ber sacht, dass der Gat-te nicht vom Schlaf er-wacht.
But more soft-ly, for my sake, That the hus-band
Ja nur lei-se still und sacht, dass der Gat-te
But more soft-ly, for her sake, That the hus-band
Ja nur lei-se still und sacht, dass der Gat-te
1.
does not wake,
nicht er-wacht
2.
does not wake.
nicht er-wacht
does not wake,
nicht er-wacht
2. All I
2. Was ich
does not wake.
nicht er-wacht

6173-191

170
170.
Allegro oppassionato.
(passionately)
R
Fr
B
Don't deny me, Do not try me.
Lass' Dir sa - gen, lass' dir kla - gen
No!
Nein!
There is some one by me.
Ich darf es nicht wa - gen!
Come more near, On me re - ly - ing.
Komm' doch nä - her im - mer nä - her!
No! Some one may be spy - ing
Nein, ich fürch-te die Spä - her!
But one kiss, sweet and dear. Do not of me have such fear.
Einen Kuss, sa - ge „Ja," sei nicht sprö - de, blei - be da!
Do not
Nicht so

R
come quite so near, For my hus - - - band is
laut, nicht so nah, denn mein Gat - - - te ist
f
R
here. Not so loud, not so near, Not so loud, not so near, For my
da! Nicht so laut, nicht so nah, nicht so laut, nicht so nah, denn mein
Fr
B
Just one kiss, soft and dear, Just one kiss, soft and dear, Do not
Ei-nen Kuss, sa-ge "Ja;" ei-nen Kuss, sa-ge "Ja!" Sei nicht
p
ff
R
hus - - - band is here.
Gat - - - - te ist da!
Fr
B
have a - - - ny fear.
spröd blei - - - be da!
ff con forza.

№ 14. Couplets.
Moderato.
FRA BOMBARDA.
PIANO.
Fine.
1. In Spring-time, oh, I love to feel The gen-tle zeph-yrs play-ing; In Sum-mer, gen-tle o-dors steal From sweet rose bush-es stray-ing. In Au-tumn, then the
2. At morn-ing I a-ri-ding go, And hunt-ing knife I car-ry; At noon-time I move on more slow, And at the ta-ble tar-ry. At eve-ning I can
3. I know ye tease through out the year, By mill-ion whims un-fold-ing, I know that it is quite se-vere, When once you start a-scold-ing; And when you get to
1. Im Früh-ling da ent-zü-cken mich die Lau-en mil-den Lüf-te; im Som-mer son-ge ger-ne ich der Ro-sen sü-sse Düf-te. Im Herbst er-quickt mich
2. Des Mor-gens reit' ich gern hi-naus, im grü-nen Wald zu ja-gen; zu Mit-tag pfleg' ich dann im Haus der Sor-ge für den Ma-gen. Des A-bends gold'-ner
3. Wohl quält Ihr uns durch's gan-ze Jahr, mit Mil-li-o-nen Lau-nen; Ihr braucht die Zun-ge wun-der-bar als Waf-fe, s'ist zum Stau-nen! Die wird von früh bis

173
grapes they grow, Their juice in Win - ter warms me so; But
sit at wine, And in the night have dreams di - vine; But
show your claws, Your tongue wags on with out a pause, But
Trau - ben - blut, im Win - ter wärmt mich Flam - men - gluth! Je -
Wein mir lacht und sü - sse Träu - me bei der Nacht; Doch
spät ge - wetzt, da - mit sich ja nicht Rost an - setzt! Doch
pp
f
circled by my sweetheart's arm, The whole year pass - es snug. and
sweet - er bliss than all these sips, I find in love - ly wom - an's
what is such a fault as this, If at the end you give a
doch in hol - der Frau - en Arm, da ist durch's gan - ze Jahr mir
sü - ssern Traum zu je - der Stund' weckt mir ein hol - der Frau - en-
was ist ta - ge - lang Ver - druss dann ge - gen ei - nen einz' - gen
fz
Molto moderato.
warm. Wom - an, Wom - an! ah you are all I wish and
lips. Wom - an, Wom - an! ah you are all I wish and
kiss? Wom - an, Wom - an! ah you are all I wish and
warm! Wei - ber, Wei - ber! Ach Ihr seid mei - ne Lust und
mund. Wei - ber, Wei - ber! Ach Ihr seid mei - ne Lust und
kuss? Wei - ber? Wei - ber? Ach Ihr seid mei - ne Lust und
p
pp
f
rit.
Moderato I.
need.
need. Woman, Woman, You are highest bliss in - deed.
need. Wei - ber, Wei - ber, mei - ne höch - ste See - lig - keit!
Freud'!
Freud'!
Freud'!
f
p
colla parte.
fp
D.S. al Fine.

Nº 15. Ensemble.

6173 - 191

From out the under world we come To bear a warning to your home.
Wir stei-gen aus der Un - ter-welt; Zur Warnung sind wir her be-stellt!
Halloh! Hurrah! Imps come faster, To your master, Tell the secrets now of Hell.
Halloh! Hussah! Komt, ihr Geister, folgt den Meister! Malt die Höllen - stra-fen aus;
cresc.
ff
tr.
Dan-te told them, now behold them, As to you we of them tell Beelzebub! Beelzebub! A
wie sie Dan-te längst schon kannte, malt sie zu der Sün - der Graus! Bel-ze-bub! Bel - ze-bub! Du
p
nice cou-ple here we know Who will go, Who will go to meet you down be-low.
Herr-scher der Fin-ster-niss! Wie-der ist, wie-der ist ein Pär-chen dir ge-wiss!

You will turn them, and will burn them In your o-ven, warm and red. You will toast them,
Vie-le O-pfer sind ver-fal-len dei-nen Gluthen weh, o weh! Sie ver-fal-len
And will roast them, For you smile when people wed.
dei-nen Kral-len, wie es üb-lich durch die Eh'!
CASTR.
Come closer now my
Komt nä-her nur her-
friends, That An-ge-lo may hear. That An-ge-lo may hear.
ein, dass An-ge-lo Euch hört! dass An-ge-lo Euch hört!
SPARAC.
Don't mind dis-turb-ing them, Come sing it yet more
Nicht scha-den kañ's führ-wahr, wenn Ihr das Pärchen
near, Come sing it yet more near.
stört, wenn Ihr das Pärchen stört!

CHOR of A.
ff
An-ge-lo hear what your friends have to say, Since you in wedlock are land-ing.
An-ge-lo! Hör', dei-ne Freun-de sind da! Hör' uns, und merk' uns're Wor-te
Think what the po-et dis-cerned one day, Up-on the
Denk' der di-vi-na Com-me-di-a! der Inschrift
gates of Sheol standing:
an der Höllen-pforte:
Maestoso.
L'istesso tempo.
Vai ch'en-tra-te og-ni speranza la-
scia-te! 'Twere better that you ne'er had birth, For marriage is a Hell on Earth.
Ver-lo-ren bist du, weh, o weh! Die Höll' auf Erden ist die Eh'
ANGELO.
No!
Nein!
marcato
pp

Allegro appassionato.
Friends you wholly are mis-ta - ken, 'Tis a Pa - ra-dise of
Freun - de schmähet nicht die E - he, denn sie ist das Pa-ra
rest; Such as Dan-te Alighi - e - ri Promised on - ly to the
dies; wie es Dan-te A-li-ghi - e - ri einst den Se - li-gen ver-
blest.
biess!
RITA.
Friends you whol-ly are mis-tak - en,
Freun - de schmähet nicht die E - he,
'Tis a Pa - ra-dise of rest, Such as Dan-te A-li-ghi-
denn sie ist das Pa - ra - dies, wie es Dan-te A-li-ghi-
e - ri Promised on - ly to the blest.
e - ri einst den Se - li-gen ver - biess!

RITA.
ANGELO.
Bliss with wedlock has its birth,
nein, die Eh' ist See_lig_keit
ff
You now shall find a Hell on earth,
Der Höl_le seid Ihr Beid'ge_weiht,
You now shall find a Hell on
der Höl_le seid Ihr Beid'ge_
ff
ffz
p
ffz
R
A
Bliss with wedlock has its birth, with wedlock has its birth.
nein, die Eh' ist Se_ligkeit, die Eh' ist See_lig_keit!
earth,
weiht,
You both will find a Hell on earth.
der Höl_le seid Ihr Beid'ge_weiht!
Allegro moderato.
Hear the warn_ing we bring,
Schweigt u_hört un_sern Chor!
We of your fate now will
Und seht Euch vor, seht Euch
ff
p
ff
p

SPARACANI.
Be calm! It shall be
Geduld! In Kurzem
CASTRUCCI.
pp
Two hours we certainly shall need, These for the rescue must be given!
Zwei Stunden Musse haben wir um sei ne Rettung kühn zu wagen!
done with speed and you from Paradise be driven!
wer den wir dich aus dem Pa-ra-dies ver-ja-gen!
Hear the song it don't take
Hort den Chor, und seht Euch
long!
Vivace, non troppo.
ff
fz

181.
Artist Solo.
You think she'll for an An - gel pass? Oh what a stu - pid
Du glaubst, sie wird dein En - gel sein? Du Thor, was fällt dir
ass. Too soon your joy will take its flight, your an - gel sweet, then will bite, you'll
ein? Gar bald der sü - sse Wahn zerreisst, dein En - gel kratzt dich u. beisst - ! Di-
find your joy has some alloy. The mot - to you must fear "Lasciate agni sper-
reckt und schnell fahrt in die Höll; Ihr Beid; durch Dunm, Dick - ! La - scia - te og - ni spe-
All the artists.
- an - za" Leave hope behind, Ye who enter here," Las - ci - ate agni sper - an - za" Leave hope be-
ran - za Lasst alles Hof - fen draussen zu - rück - ! La - scia - te og - ni spe - ran - za! Lasst alles
SPARA.
CASTR.
hind, ye who enter here"
Hof fen draussen zu rück

182
match has al-ways got some flame You'll learn now all the same - The fire will come from
Fe - ge-feu-er ist die Eh', das glüht und sprüht, o, weh ! Die Frau heizt ein so
your fond dame, She'll often scold you and blame, And when to add to all your woe, her
viel sie kann, zu kühl wird sonst ihr der Mann. Schürt dann die Schwieger mut - ter auch die
moth-er shall ap-pear - : Las-ci - ate ogni spe-ran - za! Leave hope be-hind ye who enter
Gluth noch mit Ge-schick - : La-scia - te og-ni spe-ran-za! Lasst alles Hof - fen draussen zu-
Chorus of Artists.
Las-ci - ate ogni spe-ran - za! Leave hope be-hind ye who enter here.
Las-cia - te og-ni spe-ran - za! Lasst alles Hof - fen draussen zu-rück
here
rück
And horn - ed dev - ils
Ge - horn - te Teu - fel

183.
in a row: Will set your life a-glow - , And by and bye you stupid elf you'll
dreh'n im Kreis den Mann dem furchtbar heiss ihm sprossen selbst der Hör-ner zwei und
two horns carry yourself ; To drive you wild comes child on child. Your fate will be se-
schwindlich und ihm da bei -! Komt dann geschwind noch Kind auf Kind und kront das E - he -
vere - - , Las-ci - ate ogni Sper-an -za, Leave hope behind, Ye who enter here . Las-
glück - ! La-scia - te og-ni spe-ran -za lasst, Al-les hof - fen drausen zu-ruck - ! La
-ci - ate ogni sper-an - za, leave hope be-hind all ye who shall en - ter here!
scia - te og-ni-spe-ran - za lasst Al - les hof - fen draussen zu-ruck, zu-ruck!
f
p
fz
ff

Allegro agitato.
pp
cresc.
RITA.
f
Our love they would sever, They tear thee from me; I'll stay by thee ev-er, I'll die now with thee. Oh list to my pleading, We twain can-not part, Oh be not un-heed - - - - - ing and crush not my
Man will dich mir rau-ben, man reisst dich von mir. Ich kann es nicht glauben, ich ster-be mit dir! O las-set Euch sa-gen, er-hö-ret mein Fleh'n! Nicht sollt Ihr es wa - - - - - gen, es darf nicht ge-
fz
p
cresc.
f

R
heart, Our love they would sev-er, They'd tear thee from me. I'll
ANGELO
FRA BOMB.
Who dares to con-tra-dict me, No ri-val here brook
SPARAC.
All
CASTR.
Such
CHOR of ARTISTS.
We'll rise a-gainst the ty-rant, This deed we will not bear, We'll not stand
stay by thee e-ver, I'll die now with thee!
kann es nicht glau-ben, ich ster-be mit dir!
A
stay by thee e-ver, I'll die now for thee!
kann es nicht glau-ben doch muss ich von dir!
Fr B
I; All hope is past The die is cast So let the traitor die! Off to the headsman, stay not
S
hopes gone by And he must die!
geb' - ne Müh' es bleibt da-bei!
P
Ty-ran-ny we will not bear, A res-cue dare!
dul-den wir die Ty-ran-nei, die Fre-vel-that!
C of A
by and see him die, A res-cue now for him pre-pare!

36.
R
No, oh No! It is not
Nein, o nein! Das kañ nicht
A
No, oh No!
Nein, o nein!
Fr. B
near. The hour is here. The hour is here.
zeit! Schon ist es Zeit! Schon ist es Zeit!
C
'Tis two hours yet. No, oh No! It is not
Zwei Stun-den noch! Nein, o nein! Das kañ nicht
C of A
No, oh No! It is not
Nein, o nein! Das kañ nicht
Lento.
so!
sein!
Can it be so? Is it true? A-
Ist es möglich? Was ge-schah? Die
SPARAC.
Can it be so? Is it true? A-
Ist es möglich? Was ge-schah? Die
so!
sein!
so! Can it be so? Is it true? A-
sein! Ist es möglich? Was ge-schah? Die

187.
187
Allegro giocoso
R
-las what can we do!
Stunde, sie ist da!
Angelo!
An-gelo!
A
-las what can we do!
Stunde, sie ist da!
All's lost now!
Ver-lo-ren!
(Bells ring behind Scene.)
S
-las what can we do!
Stunde, sie ist da!
C
C of A
-las what can we do!
Stunde, sie ist da!
pp rit.
pp
SOPR.
GENERAL CHORUS.
TEN.
BASS.
Ring far and wide
Fei-er-ge-läut!
Hap-piest
Fest-licher
bells!
Klang!
Your
Fröh
chim-ing
-li-cher
tells
Sang
Glad Whitsun-
Pfingsten ist

188
158.
R
A
S
C
C
of
A
CHOR
f Flo-rence shout for Joy Our duke has come To li-be-rate his home. Flo-
Pfingsten in Flo-renz! Die Ret-ter nah'n, der Herzog rückt her-an!
f Flo-rence shout for Joy Our duke has come To li-be-rate his home.
Pfingsten in Flo-renz! Die Ret-ter nah'n, der Herzog rückt her-an!
f Flo-rence shout for Joy Our duke has come To li-be-rate his home.
Pfingsten in Flo-renz! Die Ret-ter nah'n, der Herzog rückt her-an!
-tide! Flo-
heut'! Pfing
-rence shout for Joy!
-sten in Flo-renz!
Florence shout for Joy!
Pfingsten in Flo-renz!
Florence shout for Joy!
Pfingsten in Flo-renz!
-rence what Joy!
-sten ist heut'!

№ 16. Finale.

RITA. ANGELO.
PIANO.
The Whit-sun-tide Gave groom and bride All
Das Pfingst-ge-läut, es brach-te heut' uns
joy and hap-pi-ness. The gloom is past, And now at last Comes peace our fond hearts to
Glück und Se-lig-keit! Nach ban-ger Nacht der Mor-gen tagt, Ge-fahr und Leid sind ver-
bless An end has come to Ty-rant's might, And no relief he'll find! La-
jagt! Zu End' ist Fra Bom-bar-da's Macht ge-stürzt die Re-pub-lik! La-
FRA BOMB.
FORTEBR.
An end has come to all my might And no relief he'll find! La-
Zu End' ist lei-der uns're Macht ge-stürzt die Re-pub-lik! La-
SPARAC.
CASTR.
An end has come to Ty-rant's might And no relief he'll find! La-
Zu End' ist Fra Bom-bar-da's Macht ge-stürzt die Re-pub-lik! La-
GENERAL CHORUS.
An end has come to Ty-rant's might And no relief he'll find! La-
Zu End' ist Fra Bom-bar-da's Macht ge-stürzt die Re-pub-lik! La-

scia-te og-ni spe-ran-za! All hope now he must leave for be - hind! La - scia-te og-ni spe -
Lasst Al-les Hof-fen draussen zu - rück!
scia-te og-ni spe-ran-za! All hope now I must leave for be - hind! La - scia-te og-ni spe -
Lasst Al-les Hof-fen draussen zu - rück!
scia-te og-ni spe-ran-za! All hope now he must leave for be - hind! La - scia-te og-ni spe -
Lasst Al-les Hof-fen draussen zu - rück!
ff
ran - za! All hope now he must leave for be - hind.
Lasst Al-les Hof-fen draussen zu-rück!
ran - za! All hope now I must leave for be - hind.
Lasst Al-les Hof-fen draussen zu-rück!
ran - za! All hope now he must leave for be - hind.
Lasst Al-les Hof-fen draussen zu-rück!
ff
fff
End of the Opera.

Zeltfracht Medien GmbH
Ferdinand-Jühlke-Straße 7
99095 Erfurt, Deutschland
produktsicherheit@kolibri360.de